Succeeding with Your University Essay

Succeeding with Your University Essay

A step-by-step handbook

John Biggam

 Open University Press

Open University Press
McGraw-Hill Education
8th Floor, 338 Euston Road
London
England
NW1 3BH

and Two Penn Plaza, New York, NY 10121-2289, USA

First published 2020

Commissioning Editor: Vivien Antwi
Development Editor: Tom Payne
Editorial Assistant: Karen Harris
Content Product Manager: Ali Davis

A catalogue record of this book is available from the British Library

ISBN-13: 9780335248506
ISBN-10: 0335248500
eISBN: 9780335248513

Library of Congress Cataloging-in-Publication Data
CIP data applied for

Typeset by Transforma Pvt. Ltd., Chennai, India

Fictitious names of companies, products, people, characters and/or data that may be used herein (in case studies or in examples) are not intended to represent any real individual, company, product or event.

Printed in Great Britain by Bell and Bain Ltd, Glasgow

Praise page

"This book sets out everything a student needs to know to write a university essay – except the essay content, of course! It sets out information in a methodical and approachable way and highlights common misunderstandings and errors made by students, with advice on how to avoid them.

Through explicitly linking its content with current assessment structures in Higher Education, this book provides very valuable, contextualised directions for students writing essays at any level of HE."

Daisy Abbott, School of Simulation and Visualisation,
The Glasgow School of Art, UK

This book is dedicated to those working-class kids I grew up with in Balornock, Glasgow: Brennie and Kevin 'Kos' McKenna, Brian 'Brain' Grimes, Gary 'Good Times' Cunningham, Rab 'Bags I'm Alan Ladd!' McGlame, and Brian 'BoS' O'Sullivan, to name but a few. This one's for you.

This book is also dedicated to Roger Daltrey of The Who. If there is one lesson that you can take from Roger Daltrey it is this: skill will get you on the ladder, but determination will get you up it.

Brief contents

Contents

List of tables and figures

Notes on the author

John Biggam has wide-ranging experience of teaching at school, college and university level. He has published extensively in academia and is the author of the popular book *Succeeding with Your Master's Dissertation*, now in its fourth edition. He has presented at numerous prestigious conferences and regularly gives guest lectures on how to write at university level.

What's in this book and how to use it

What's in it for me?

'Write about anything you want. Make it long or short. Your choice. References are optional. Hand it in when you feel like it. Good luck, your tutor.' [25 marks]

That's the essay question that all students long to see. Or so you think, because that question would also cause you nightmares. What would happen, very quickly, is that you would inundate your tutor with an avalanche of email queries, not quite trusting your own judgement:

- What should I write about?
- How short is short?
- What do you mean by long?
- Do I get more marks if I include references?
- Do I need a bibliography?
- What is everybody else writing about?
- Is there a word limit?
- Can I write about two things?
- When's the latest I can hand it in?
- What about diagrams? It doesn't say anything about diagrams!
- How is this marked?

Then the cycle of questions would start with fellow students: 'What are you going to write about?'; 'Are you doing references? How many?', 'How long do you think you'll make it?', etc.

As you can see, such an open-ended essay question raises even more questions. It places the responsibility on you to define a subject focus and other related parameters. In effect, it's telling you to come up with the question. That's more difficult than it sounds – just ask dissertation students. If only someone would be kind enough to set the question for you – how that would make life so much easier!

That is why you should view university essay questions in a new light. They are your friend: they are focused, they ask you to perform specific tasks, in a particular way, using credible sources, in a set time frame, using so many words, in order to obtain a particular mark. However – there is always a *however* – to do what's being asked of you, you need to fine-tune your academic ears to pick up the right signals. Get your signals crossed and who knows what your essay will look like. Unfortunately, too many students do not tune in to what is playing right in their ear. That is what holds some students back from delivering a great university essay each and every time. This discrepancy has very little, if anything, to do with natural intelligence, if there is such a thing; it is about the acquisition of knowledge and the application of knowledge.

Writing a university essay is primarily a matter of technique. This is good news because technique can be taught. Unfortunately, many students remain unaware of the technique of university essay-writing and continue nervously to submit guesswork. And that is where this book comes in. This book teaches you, in five easy steps:

1 How to deconstruct an essay question.
2 How to structure an essay.
3 How to write an introduction.
4 How to write the main body.
5 How to conclude an essay.

Other important topics covered include: the written language, referencing and student feedback. As a result, you will have a better understanding of the language that tutors often find when marking essays, and the language that they would prefer to see; you will learn how to reference properly (full reference templates are included for Harvard Referencing); and you will know what to do when you get formal feedback from your tutor.

In short, you will face the ubiquitous university essay question from an informed position. Indeed, the skills that you pick up in this book – language, writing, referencing – will still be there for you when you're retired and contemplating writing your memoirs.

How to use this book

This book has been carefully structured to meet the needs of students writing university essays. Here's how:

* *Chapters 1 and 2* are on the language that students ought to use in essay-writing. Chapter 1 teaches you the formal stuff, such as how to write in paragraphs (a common failing evidenced in student essays), as well as covering punctuation, the differences between British and American spelling (an increasing issue in this internet age), numbers in essays, and using verbs to good effect. Chapter 2 is more concerned with the fancy stuff, the subtleties of written language that, as a university student, you really ought to know

about, such as alliteration and metaphors, and the words that students conflate. Both chapters are filled with explanatory examples. Read these chapters first – even if you think you are conversant in written English there will be something in it that you will find of use. If nothing else, it will refresh old skills in a new setting: university essays.

- Next, there is a crucial chapter on referencing (*Chapter 3*). Referencing is a core activity in academia. You will learn how to cite sources in the body of your essay and, equally important, how to create a reference list at the end of your essay. A complete referencing template for the Harvard author–date system is included for your convenience. Do not miss this chapter!

- *Chapter 4* highlights two key concepts: (1) that there is a hierarchy to learning (from the acquisition of basic knowledge to the ability to evaluate); and (2) that this hierarchy is also reflected in university essay questions through the use of *action words* (e.g. list, outline, describe, explain, analyse and assess). These concepts are crucial to understanding how to answer an essay question.

- *Chapters 5–9* – the heart of the book – take you through each of the five steps towards how to write a university essay. Step 1 (Chapter 5) tells you how to deconstruct your essay question; Step 2 (Chapter 6), how to create a roadmap (i.e. a structure) for your essay; Step 3 (Chapter 7), how to write your introduction; Step 4 (Chapter 8), how to write the main body; and Step 5 (Chapter 9), how to conclude your essay. After a while, taking these steps will become second nature.

- *Chapter 10* clarifies the different types of student feedback and the criteria that good feedback should meet and offers advice on what to do when you get formal feedback on graded essays. Read this chapter before you get your feedback – that way, you will be in a better position to view feedback as a learning opportunity and exploit it accordingly.

- *Chapter 11*, the last chapter, walks you through some quick tips for best practice when writing a university essay – use this as a handy reference point whenever you have an essay due.

Each chapter ends with a helpful Summary of Key Points. In addition, common mistakes made by students when writing university essays will be highlighted as follows:

 A common student mistake

Throughout this book, common mistakes made by students with regard to essay writing will be highlighted. For instance, if it is necessary to warn you about bad practice related to referencing literature, then this book will go on to indicate errors that are commonly made by students when they try and reference works that they have read.

This book is designed to help students succeed in writing university essays of note. After reading this book, you should be able to banish those *scriptophobia* blues and embrace university essay questions without fear.

Summary of key points

- University essays create unnecessary anxiety among many students.
- Answering essay questions is more a craft than an art – it's a matter of technique.
- By demystifying the writing process and providing easy-to-follow steps, reinforced with copious examples of good practice, this book teaches you the technique of answering university essay questions.
- Succeed in your submissions by following the chapters in the order recommended in this book: by learning about the language that we use, referencing, the role played by action words, the stages of writing an essay, and how to deal with feedback.

PART **1**

Grasping the basics:
From language to learning

1 The language that you use: The formal stuff

Paragraphs: The building blocks
Punctuation
Spelling: British English versus American English
Writing numbers
Useful verbs

The purpose of language is to facilitate communication. To aid in this task, we use different styles of language – called 'registers' – for different situations. For example, lovers will share an intimate language; a neighbour will be friendly but not assume intimacy; a shopkeeper will be friendly but business-like; a doctor giving advice adheres to a formal, consultative approach; a lawyer will be formal and factual; with friends we adopt a casual, conversational tone, where slang words and abbreviations, in speech and text, are accepted practice. Register is to do with appropriate use of language in a given situation. To communicate effectively, you need to use the register that is conventionally appropriate to a given situation. Accordingly, university students are expected to submit essays that display a formal tone, one commensurate with academic practice and Standard English. This chapter will look at these academic conventions, starting with the building blocks of any academic essay: paragraphs.

Paragraphs: The building blocks

An essay consists of a collection of paragraphs. A common error by students is to mistake a sentence for a paragraph and, for the most part, pepper their essay with disjointed, stand-alone sentences that, in turn, act as assertions rather than arguments. For example, this is not an acceptable paragraph in an academic essay:

Capitalism is a modern form of slavery that exploits the many for the benefit of the few, using the cloak of meritocracy and the carrot of greed.

Short, sharp, assertive sentences, however interesting and informative, are better suited to newspaper articles, where column inches dictate the form of the message. University essays require a different format, one made up of conventional paragraphs. So, what passes for a paragraph in academia? A paragraph is a focused unit of discourse dealing with an identified topic. As such, the first sentence of the paragraph is the *topic sentence* (i.e. it introduces the topic to be addressed in the paragraph). The following are examples of introductory topic sentences:

> Capitalism is a modern form of slavery.
>
> Plagiarism is a serious problem in universities.
>
> I love walking.
>
> The verdict of 'not proven' serves no useful purpose.
>
> What is meant by *existentialism*?
>
> What is the difference between *disinterested* and *uninterested*?

In effect, your topic sentence is preparing the reader (i.e. your marker) for the focus of your paragraph. It states unequivocally: *this is what I am about to discuss in this paragraph.* This means that you must concentrate exclusively on addressing that topic, and only that topic. In other words, anything that is unrelated to your paragraph topic should be ruthlessly jettisoned. Here is an example of a paragraph that starts well but inserts irrelevant material (in bold for emphasis):

> I love walking. The exercise is good for me. I exercise at the local gym and the subscription rates are good but walking is free. **The staff at the gym are nice – Tom in particular (he likes to crack jokes!).** When I walk, I can go places that are not accessible by car or public transport. **I have a car but I spend too much time cleaning it!** Walking also gives me time to think on my own without interruptions. And, best of all, I love walking deep into the countryside where, after a hearty picnic, I can drift asleep on a soft grassy slope on a warm summer's day. **Summer always seems the shortest season of the year.** Nothing beats a good walk.

The topic sentence is 'I love walking', so the reader expects to find out why the writer loves walking. The text in bold, although interesting, is irrelevant. In an academic essay, additional material not relevant to your essay is called 'padding'. It distracts the reader, eats into your word count, prevents you from devoting more time and energy on core issues, gets you no extra marks, and indeed may cost you marks. Bin it.

Furthermore, the use of the personal pronoun 'I' grates on the academic teeth of those who write in British English; if you write in American English, then its use will not offend American eyes. In academic (British) English, there is the tacit pretence that the author dare not peek out from the veneer of objective scholarship lest a real person is exposed. Sticking with that tradition, the 'I love walking' paragraph, with the first-person singular removed, as well as the padding, now reads:

> What is not to love about walking? The exercise is good for you. Even if subscription rates at the local gym are affordable, walking is free. Walking allows the opportunity to go places not accessible by private car or public transport. It also gives you time to think, away from everyday interruptions. Best of all, after a long walk, deep in the countryside, and following a hearty picnic, there is the solitary pleasure of falling asleep on a soft grassy slope on a warm summer's day. Nothing beats a good walk.

You may have noticed a concluding sentence in the altered paragraph above: 'Nothing beats a good walk'. A concluding sentence is not compulsory but, in this example, it underlines the message of the discussed topic. If you decide to have a concluding sentence at the end of a paragraph, then you can simply rearrange the words of your opening sentence (see Table 1.1) or you can try and capture what you have just written in a more informative way (see Table 1.2). The closing sentence is not an opportunity to raise another point. If you have a different point to make, then make it in a different paragraph.

Table 1.1 Repetitive closing paragraph sentences

Opening sentences	*Repetitive* closing sentences
1 What is not to love about walking?	1 Walking is an activity to be loved.
2 Plagiarism is a serious problem in universities.	2 For those reasons, plagiarism is a serious issue in universities.
3 The verdict of 'not proven' serves no useful purpose.	3 And that is why the verdict of 'not proven' serves no useful purpose.

Table 1.2 Informative closing paragraph sentences

Opening sentences	*Informative* closing sentences
1 What is not to love about walking?	1 Nothing beats walking.
2 Plagiarism is a serious problem in universities.	2 Clearly, universities have a long way to go before they can solve the problem of plagiarism.
3 The verdict of 'not proven' serves no useful purpose.	3 The verdict of 'not proven' is an anachronism that ought to be removed.

There is no definitive rule for the number of sentences in a paragraph. That is your choice. However, if you make it too few, then your essay might start to resemble a newspaper article; too many, and it will look like a mini essay, with the added risk of boring the reader. Short paragraphs, although punchy, tend to lack depth. Then again, if your paragraph is stretching to half a page, you really ought to consider breaking it up into several paragraphs. A balance is required, one that achieves the task of addressing the topic sentence in a meaningful way but avoids the academic's addiction to waffle.

Transitional words are used to link paragraphs and even sentences within paragraphs. They can also be used to show a logical flow and conclude paragraphs and the essay itself. Examples of transitional words include: *accordingly, furthermore, on the other hand,* and *therefore.* You might find it more helpful to see these linking words under appropriate thematic headings (Table 1.3).

If you want to enumerate a finite number of points, then you can make use of the formula, 'First, . . . Secondly, . . . Thirdly, . . .':

> There are three reasons why Labour won the election. First, they had a charismatic leader. Secondly, their policies had wide appeal. Thirdly, the Conservatives ran a poor campaign.

If the points to be made are substantial, then you can devote a separate paragraph to each point ('Secondly, . . .'). To indicate that you are concluding your points, you could precede the final point with 'Lastly, . . .' or 'Finally, . . .'. That

Table 1.3 Transitional words and phrases according to themes

Agreement	Difference	Logical flow/concluding
Additionally; again; also; along with; and; as well as; besides; by the same token; certainly; coupled with; equally; equally important; even more so; further; furthermore; in addition; in conjunction with; indeed; in fact; in like manner; in other words; in similar fashion; in the same way; likewise; moreover; more than that; not to mention; on top of; over and above; plus; similarly; together with; too; undoubtedly.	Against this; all the same; alternatively; although; anyhow; at the same time; at variance; be that as it may; but; despite that; despite the fact; even if; even so; even though; for all that; granting all this; however; in any case; in contrast; in opposition; in spite of that; nevertheless; nonetheless; notwithstanding; on the contrary; on the other hand; regardless; still; that as may be; though; yet.	Accordingly; all in all; all things considered; as a result of; as shown above; briefly; by and large; concluding; consequently; correspondingly; finally; for that (those) reason(s); given these points; hence; in any case; in any event; in brief; in conclusion; in light of; in the final analysis; in short; in summary; on balance; on the whole; overall; therefore; to summarise; to sum up; thus.

said, if you get to 'Fourteenthly' before arriving at 'Finally', then it is likely that your reader has given up the ghost and gone on holiday.

Not everyone agrees on how to write First, Secondly, Thirdly, etc. Some argue that it is perfectly acceptable to write First, Second, Third, etc., while others insist that, for consistency, there is nothing wrong with Firstly, Secondly, Thirdly, etc. Traditional grammarians, however, tend to agree that the grammatically correct form is First, Secondly, Thirdly, etc.

Punctuation

Punctuation is the use of marks to clarify meaning in a sentence. Typical examples include the full stop, the comma, the colon, and the semi-colon. Punctuation is not grammar but it is the glue that holds a sentence together.

The full stop (.)

In British English, the end of a sentence is marked by a *full stop*. In American English, the same baseline mark is called a *period*.

- A full stop normally indicates the end of a statement, such as:

    Kay thanked everyone for their gifts.

- A full stop is also used when a term is shortened:

    i.e. (A shortened version of the Latin term *id est*, meaning *that is*, translated as *in other words*.)

    e.g. (Latin term *exempli gratia*, meaning *for example*.)

    etc. (Latin term *et cetera*, meaning *and so forth*, translated as *and so on*. It is used where the continuing list of items is so obvious that they need not be stated [see 'First', 'Secondly', 'Thirdly', etc.].)

Not all abbreviations use a full stop (e.g. MSc, MPhil and PhD are regularly seen without a full stop).

If a sentence ends in an abbreviated term that itself uses a full stop, then there is no need to include another full stop to conclude the sentence:

    The grocery shop had a colourful display of fruit and vegetables: apples, oranges, bananas, carrots, peas, cauliflowers, etc.

Incidentally, do you know the difference between an abbreviation and an acronym? An abbreviation – from Latin *brevis* meaning *short* – is a shortened version of a word or group of words; an acronym is a pronounceable word that is formed from the initials of a group of words. Thus, NHS is an abbreviation – it's not pronounceable, at least not sober – of National Health Service, whereas NASA is an acronym of National Aeronautics and Space Administration.

- When brackets start and end a sentence, the full stop appears inside the closing bracket, not outside:

  > Full stops tend to conclude a sentence. (This sentence shows how to use a full stop in a stand-alone sentence that is enclosed within brackets.)

- Similarly, when quoting a source, and where the quotation itself ends in a full stop, then there is no need for an additional full stop to be placed after the closing quotation mark:

  > As Thomson (2018, p.12) famously quipped: 'I never mistake silence for listening.'

- However, if the quotation is partial and does not end in a full stop, then do not include one. In which case, the full stop appears outside the closing quotation mark:

  > No one really knows what Riley meant when he used the phrase, 'that sort of thing'.

The comma (,)

Commas are used in a number of ways in a sentence:

- To separate items in a list:

  > The wallet contained credit cards, a gym membership card, an insurance card, a bus pass, two £10 notes, and some loose change.

- After words and phrases that start a sentence, then require a slight pause for effect, such as *yet, nevertheless, indeed, however, on the other hand, to begin with, on the contrary*, etc.:

  > However, Sartre's view of existentialism differed markedly from Heidegger's.
  >
  > To begin with, there is no agreed definition of freedom.
  >
  > Still, grammar is worth fighting for.
  >
  > Accordingly, the elderly ought to be treated with dignity.

- In direct speech, before the closing quotation mark:

  > 'I hate school,' said Louise.

- In direct speech, before the opening quotation mark:

  > 'Yes,' I said, 'I will marry you.'

- Commas are also used to separate *clauses*, but clauses are covered in Chapter 2.

The Oxford Comma (, and)

The Oxford Comma, originating from Oxford University Press, places a comma before the 'and' at the end of a list:

> In the waiting room sat her husband, the postman, and the village drunk.

The purpose of the Oxford Comma is to avoid ambiguity. If we removed the Oxford Comma from the previous example, then there is some confusion about how many people were in the waiting room:

> In the waiting room sat her husband, the postman and the village drunk.

From having certainty that three people sat in the waiting room (the husband, the postman, and the village drunk), there now appears to be either one person, someone's husband, who also happens to be the postman and the village drunk, or three people.

Here are two other examples, with, and then without, the Oxford Comma:

> The child worshipped her parents, God, and Pocahontas.
> The child worshipped her parents, God and Pocahontas.

In the first example, the Oxford Comma makes it clear that the child worshipped three entities: her parents, God, and Pocahontas. In the second example, the absence of the Oxford Comma means that the child worshipped her parents, whom rightly or wrongly she believes to be God and Pocahontas.

Including an Oxford Comma at best removes ambiguity and at worse does no harm. Here is an example of a redundant Oxford Comma, with zero ill-effect:

> On his plate were sausages, eggs, bacon, tomatoes, and black pudding.
> On his plate were sausages, eggs, bacon, tomatoes and black pudding.

In this case, there is no difference as far as ambiguity goes with or without the Oxford Comma, so no harm done. If you start to use the Oxford Comma, it will very quickly become second nature. If it is not required, then the world will not stop spinning; if it is required, then you have removed a possible ambiguity.

Clauses, commas, and interrupters

A clause in a sentence consists of a noun (person, place, or thing) or pronoun (something that stands for a noun, e.g. he, she, it, they) and a verb (a doing word, e.g. love):

> I [pronoun] enjoy [verb] writing [noun].

A sentence can have more than one clause:

> I enjoy writing and I love presentations.

This example consists of two clauses separated by the conjunction 'and'. A clause can stand alone as a sentence in its own right (e.g. *I enjoy writing* makes sense as a sentence in its own right, as does *I love presentations*). The easiest way to think of clauses is to think of the parts of a sentence that, when you take them out, can form a stand-alone sentence.

A subordinate clause is a second clause that is dependent on the main clause:

> I ran when the dog barked.

In this case, *I ran* is the main clause and *when the dog barked* is the subordinate clause. Subordinate clauses usually don't make sense as a sentence on their own. The main clause, *I ran*, makes sense on its own, whereas *when the dog barked* doesn't.

A subordinate clause can also appear before the main clause. When that happens, both the subordinate clause and the main clause are usually separated by a comma:

> When the dog barked, I ran.

> Above all, I love curries.

As well as appearing either before or after a main clause, a subordinate clause can interrupt a main clause. When that happens, the subordinate clause is called an *interrupter*. Interrupters are sandwiched between two commas. The text in bold in the following examples illustrates the interrupting subordinate clauses:

> Thomson, **despite his earlier position**, agreed with Barnes.

> Jacqueline, **without speaking to anyone**, left the room.

> His theory, **on closer inspection**, lacks coherence.

The Oxford Comma can also be used to good effect with subordinate clauses, particularly with interrupters. Remember, an Oxford Comma is a comma that appears before an 'and' at the end of a sentence in order to remove any ambiguity. Let's start with a simple sentence that lacks clarity. We will then insert an Oxford Comma to improve the clarity. Then, lastly, introduce an interrupter to see how that affects the Oxford Comma:

> Ambiguous sentence: I love my dogs, D. H. Lawrence and Bruce Springsteen.

With Oxford Comma:

> I love my dogs, D. H. Lawrence, and Bruce Springsteen.

Interrupter:

> I love my dogs, D. H. Lawrence, and, **above all**, Bruce Springsteen.

The first sentence – *I love my dogs, D. H. Lawrence and Bruce Springsteen* – might suggest that D. H. Lawrence and Bruce Springsteen are the dogs that are loved. The Oxford Comma clarifies that three things are loved: the dogs, D. H. Lawrence, and Bruce Springsteen. The interrupter – *above all* – is enclosed between two commas for emphasis.

The colon (:)

There are three main occasions when a colon is used:

- To introduce a list:

  > Making Scottish tablet requires a number of simple ingredients: caster sugar, butter, condensed sweetened milk, milk, and vanilla extract.

- To introduce a quotation:

  > As Churchill said: 'If you're going through Hell, keep going.'

- To explain or expand on something:

  > I hate school: it's so boring.

  > I love curries: the spicy aroma, the exotic flavours, the texture and, best of all, it makes me think of home.

  > The Mona Lisa's 'smile' is the cause of much debate: some claim that it is an expression of unequivocal happiness, while others insist that it is forced and reveals an inner sadness.

- A fourth use, which is really an extension of the previous point but one that occurs so often in student essays that it merits comment on its own, occurs when a figure, table, or diagram is being introduced:

  > As shown in Figure 5.1 below:

  > Table 8.2 illustrates the typical life cycle of a plant:

The semi-colon (;)

There are two ways to use a semi-colon:

- To separate items in a list wherein a comma appears in one or more of the items (otherwise a comma is used to separate the items). The first example shows a list using commas; the second example shows a list using semi-colons:

> He placed his favourite books on the table: Sons and Lovers, The Catcher in the Rye, Catch-22, The Grapes of Wrath, and A Farewell to Arms.

> He placed his favourite books on the table: Sons and Lovers, by D. H. Lawrence; The Catcher in the Rye, by J. D. Salinger; Catch-22, by Joseph Heller; The Grapes of Wrath, by John Steinbeck; and A Farewell to Arms, by Ernest Hemingway.

If commas were used in the second example, instead of semi-colons, then the job of identifying the separate items in the list would become that much harder:

> He placed his favourite books on the table: Sons and Lovers, by D. H. Lawrence, The Catcher in the Rye, by J. D. Salinger, Catch-22, by Joseph Heller, The Grapes of Wrath, by John Steinbeck, and A Farewell to Arms, by Ernest Hemingway.

However, the requirement for at least one of the separated items to include a comma has been relaxed over time. Remember, in the context of lists, semi-colons were introduced to bring clarity. If they still do that job, even where commas would have sufficed, then there is no harm done. Thus, it is perfectly acceptable to use semi-colons in a list where commas work fine (though pedants will squirm at the very thought), as in:

> He placed his favourite books on the table: Sons and Lovers; The Catcher in the Rye; Catch-22; The Grapes of Wrath; and A Farewell to Arms.

Semi-colons have the additional advantage that they can be used for emphasis. A semi-colon is a strong pause, so if you want to emphasise your items by slowing down your readers, then by all means insert semi-colons:

> Three things depressed her: life; death; and Wittgenstein.

Rules are not there to be broken because it is cool to do so: they are there to be broken if there is good reason to do so.

- To link *complete sentences* that are closely related:

> It never stopped raining today; he hoped for sunshine tomorrow.

> [It never stopped raining today. He hoped for sunshine tomorrow.]

> Tea calmed him down; coffee made him high.

> [Tea calmed him down. Coffee made him high.]

In the following examples, the semi-colon is inappropriate because it does not link complete sentences:

> He needed a new pair of trousers; maybe black.

> ['Maybe black.' is not a complete sentence.]

Italy is beautiful; great architecture.

['Great architecture.' is not a complete sentence.]

Some students mistakenly use a comma instead of a semi-colon to separate two related sentences. This is called, rather appropriately, the *comma splice*. They write:

It never stopped raining today, he hoped for sunshine tomorrow.

Instead of:

It never stopped raining today; he hoped for sunshine tomorrow.

Avoid the comma splice, it is very annoying.
Connecting words like *and, but,* and *or* are called 'conjunctions'. They are now commonly seen, for emphasis, appearing at the start of a sentence. They can also be used immediately after a semi-colon: in lists and to link two complete, but related, sentences:

The garden was in full bloom with flowers: red and, for the first time, blue roses; shimmering bluebells; buttercups; daffodils; and, our personal favourite, tulips.

He annoys me no end; but, I love him.

The hyphen (-), the en sign (–), and the em sign (—)

The hyphen (-) is used to connect either words or numbers to form one word or number:

She was a little-known celebrity.

The colour of the sea was blue-green.

His social security number was 12-65-35-67.[1]

The en sign (–) is a horizontal sign that is longer than a hyphen. It is the length of the letter N (hence its name) and it is primarily used to indicate a range of numbers:

2016–2017

6:15–7:15 p.m.

Standing room: 6–9 people

It is also used, like the hyphen, to form a compound adjective:

Part–time workers

State–of–the–art computers

The em sign is a horizontal line (—) that is longer than the en sign. It is commonly known as a dash. It is the width of the letter M (hence its name). It is used either for parenthesis or as a pointer to a comment you wish to make:

> The boys — John and Alan — were glad to be home.
>
> The theory was sound in principle — or so everyone thought.

When the dash — or em sign if you prefer — is used to interrupt a sentence, there is the option of either using them with or without spaces:

> The boys — John and Alan — were glad to be home.
>
> The boys—John and Alan—were glad to be home.

Omitting spaces, though, may lead to some confusion, mistaking the dash for a hyphen that is attempting to form, in the previous example, the words *boys— John* and *Alan—were*.

Those are the rules about the hyphen, the en sign, and the em sign. The reality is, however, that language evolves, and that includes grammar and punctuation. In the context of university essays, it is very rare to witness the three different types of horizontal line being used. The fact is, the two most common lines used are the hyphen (typically, the minus sign) and the dash: the former to connect words (and numbers) and the latter to interrupt a sentence or to make an observation. Even if you were keen on following these rules, it is not easy to find, for example, the en sign on your word processor – especially when you are under pressure! While 'correct' English is to be applauded, evolution is a powerful persuader. You will not lose marks if you follow modern custom and practice in your institution.

The oblique (/)

The oblique is also known more commonly as the 'slash'. It is used to present alternatives:

> Each student is required to show his/her gym card.
>
> [Each student is required to show his or her gym card.]
>
> Dear Sir/Madam
>
> [Dear Sir or Madam]
>
> If/when the alarm goes off, we will make our way downstairs.
>
> [If or when the alarm goes off, . . .]

Confusingly, the oblique can also be used to stand for something that doubles up as something else. In other words, the opposite of the 'or' situation just seen:

He slept in his caravan/home.

[He slept in his caravan, which was also his home.]

He stared malevolently at his bike/torture instrument.

[He stared malevolently at his bike-cum-torture instrument.]

Don't panic, though. The context should make clear the meaning of an oblique. Less problematically, the oblique is also used to mean *per*, as in:

The salary was a generous £3,000/month.

The car was travelling at an average speed of 80 km/h.

The question mark (?)

Obviously, when asking a question. No?

The exclamation mark (!)

An exclamation is a statement expressing a strong feeling of pain, pleasure, surprise, etc. In such circumstances, an exclamation mark can be used:

I hate him!

There were chocolates everywhere!

Look, there's Billy Connolly!

An exclamation mark can also be used to emphasise a particular word, in which case it is placed within round or square brackets forming parentheses:

He said he loved (!) his job.

Multiple exclamation marks can be used for effect, usually within quotation marks as part of direct speech:

'No!!! I will not tolerate such behaviour!'

Exclamation marks are generally frowned upon in university essays. Their use suggests exaggerated excitement, normally something best left to texting between friends.

Round brackets or parentheses (( ))

Round brackets are also known, in American English, as 'parentheses'. Round brackets are used to provide the reader with additional information. There is a condition attached to using round brackets, and that is that the sentence without the additional information must make sense on its own. Here is an example of a correct usage of round brackets:

Alan snored all night (a fact he never accepted).

And here is an example of an incorrect usage of round brackets:

The Pope (and his entourage) were expected to arrive soon.

['The Pope were expected to arrive soon' is not a proper sentence on its own.]

Round brackets can even be placed in a separate sentence (the full stop then appears inside the closing bracket):

His loyalty was divided. (More on this matter later.)

Square brackets or brackets ([ ])

Square brackets are also known, in American English, simply as 'brackets'. They are used to interrupt a quotation in order to clarify something, to make clear to the reader what something is referring to:

He [the doorman] is not to blame.

The main witness [Ms Travis] was then called to give evidence.

Stevenson claims that sexism is rife in the modern world: 'too often they [women] are treated as second class citizens'.

You are not altering the source text in any way: all you are doing is attempting to clarify meaning. It is particularly irritating to witness tabloid journalists (usually football reporters) using square brackets to excess for a knowledge-able readership that has no need of the additional information:

The manager [Bob Johnson] has a lot on his plate to get our club [Crampton City] playing well at this hallowed ground [Huntersfield]. As far as contracts go, he will talk to Engelbert [Thomson] and Leonardo [Martinéz] in due course, and hopefully everything will be ready for their first game [against Bringford United].

Square brackets are also used with *sic* in a quotation. *Sic* means *thus* and it is used to indicate that you are aware that the source has made a linguistic error (usually a misspelling). It is not your job to correct the error. Hence the use of [*sic*]. Note that *sic* is italicised:

The office is closed on Tuesray [*sic*].

The party overflowed with revelers [*sic*].

The kids enjoyed there [*sic*] time at the holiday camp.

One other use of the square bracket, one that is especially pertinent to university essay writing, is when adding parentheticals inside parentheticals. This is very common with in-text referencing. For example:

> In 2015, 20% of students failed to write a successful essay (this contrasts with earlier findings that suggested 50% of students failed to write a successful essay [Strong, 2012]).

Quotation marks (' ' or " ")

When quoting someone, you can use either single quotation marks (' ') or double quotation marks (" "). The disadvantage of using single quotation marks is that if there is an apostrophe in the quotation, then there may be some confusion as to when the quotation ends:

> Rafford took the view that 'the men's behaviour was despicable'.

Whereas double quotation marks remove any confusion:

> Rafford took the view that "the men's behaviour was despicable".

British English tends to use single quotation marks, but American English favours double quotation marks. Double quotation marks appear to be winning global dominance but whichever one you choose, be consistent.

Some people don't like the use of commas or colons to introduce a quotation, but that is a matter of taste and nothing to do with rules. For instance, all the following are correct, although the first one reads more smoothly, with the commentary running seamlessly into the quotation:

> Rafford took the view that 'the men's behaviour was despicable'.

> Rafford took the view that, 'the men's behaviour was despicable'.

> Rafford took the view that: 'the men's behaviour was despicable'.

That said, a sensible approach to adopt is as follows: use a colon if the quotation starts with a capital letter; otherwise, let it run naturally as part of the sentence:

> The neighbour complained 'about the racket next door'.

> The neighbour left a note under the door: 'Please stop making so much noise.'

One last point on the use of quotation marks. If a full stop is not in the original quotation, then do not insert one in the quotation. In such a scenario, place the full stop after the quotation. For example:

> The employee wrote: 'I hereby submit my resignation.'

> [This is fine if the employee included a full stop in his resignation note.]

If not, then:

> The employee wrote: 'I hereby submit my resignation'.

Some people object to this practice and prefer that a full stop is also included before the closing quotation mark regardless of circumstance. This does not make sense. If a full stop does not exist in a partial quotation, then why include it? If you are quoting direct speech, then use your own judgement. Regardless of the position you adopt, the world will not stop turning and consistency is key.

Quotation marks are also used in direct speech (discussed earlier). Single quotations marks or double ones are your options, but whichever you choose, be consistent:

> 'You're funny,' laughed Louise.
>
> "You're funny," laughed Louise.

The apostrophe (')

The apostrophe is much abused. The apostrophe has two uses: to indicate a contraction (missing letter) and a possessive.

* *Contractions. Let's* is a contraction of 'let us'. Similarly, *don't* is a contraction of 'do not', and *it's* is a contraction of 'it is' (more on *it's* later).

Contractions introduce a conversational tone to an essay. Avoid contractions in essays. A university essay is a formal piece of prose and no place for casual language. Examples (including correct usage) can be found in Table 1.4.

Table 1.4 Contractions

Contraction	Full form
That's	That is
What's	What is
Here's	Here is
There's	There is
Won't	Will not
Haven't	Have not

In other words, in a formal university essay, don't write *don't* when you can write *do not*.

* *Possessives.* The apostrophe can be used to show possession by adding *'s* to a noun. For example, to show that a boy has a ball, we can write 'the boy's ball'. Other examples can be seen in Table 1.5.

Table 1.5 Possessives

Apostrophe example		Equivalent
The dog's tail	=	the tail belonging to the dog
The policeman's baton	=	the baton belonging to the policeman
Lewis's friends	=	friends of Lewis
The woman's dress	=	the dress belonging to the woman
The doctor's stethoscope	=	the stethoscope belonging to the doctor
Dickens's books	=	books written by Dickens

Table 1.6 Possessives for plurals

Where the plural of the noun ends in s (')	Where the plural of the noun does not end in s ('s)
The cars' occupants	The women's clothes
The boys' over-exuberance	The children's playground
Three weeks' holidays	The men's section
The girls' boyfriends	The tooth's enamel

Table 1.5 deals with possessives for singular nouns (dog, woman, policeman, doctor, Lewis, and Dickens). If the noun is plural, then a simple rule is followed: if the plural already ends in s (e.g. dogs), then it's only necessary to add an apostrophe (e.g. dogs'), otherwise an 's is added (e.g. women's).

Table 1.6 shows some examples of possessives where the plural of the noun ends in s (so only add ') and where the plural of the noun does not end in s (so add 's).

Its and it's

These two are commonly conflated by students. Let's start with *it's* first. *It's* is a contraction of *it is* or *it has*. The apostrophe does not indicate a possession at all: it signals a contraction. *Its*, on the other hand, does refer to a possession, but never uses an apostrophe (otherwise it would be impossible to distinguish the possessive *its* from the contraction *it's*). Table 1.7 offers some examples of the use of *it's* and *its*.

Here is how to tell if you are using *it's* correctly. Expand the contraction *it's* to *it is* and see if the sentence still makes sense. If it does, then you are using *it's* properly; if it doesn't make sense, then you should be using *its* (see Table 1.8).

Table 1.7   Examples of the possessive *its* and the contraction *it's*

The possessive *its*	The contraction *it's*
Its owner was never found	It's raining today
The cat licked its paw	It's devastating news
The dog wagged its tail	It's a lion!
Its days were numbered	It's not my fault

Table 1.8   Correct and incorrect use of *it's*

Correct use of *it's*	Incorrect use of *it's*
It's that time of the day again = it is that time of the day again	It's jaw was wide open = it is jaw was wide open
It's going to be a tough year = it is going to be a tough year	It's branches hung low = it is branches hung low
It's been a long day = it has been a long day	It's windows needed replacing = it is windows needed replacing

Another common mistake is to confuse plurals with possessives:

Incorrect: IOU's are not worth a jot.

Correct: IOUs are not worth a jot.

Incorrect: The student's are heading home.

Correct: The students are heading home.

Capitals

The first letter of a sentence starts with a capital letter (although poets some-times breach this convention because it is cool to do so). Days of the week start with a capital letter (Monday, Tuesday, etc.) but seasons don't (summer, autumn, winter, and spring). Other things that begin with a capital letter are:

- countries (Scotland, England, etc.);
- languages (English, Italian, etc.);
- names (John, Kay, etc.);
- festivals, holy days, and events (Christmas, Easter, Ramadan, Remembrance Day, etc.);
- historical periods (Dark Ages, Middle Ages, Enlightenment, Renaissance, etc.).

Proper nouns – i.e. the name given to a *particular* person, place, or thing (typically, an organisation) – are capitalised (Alan, Glasgow, the British Council).

For books, plays, and films, the first letter is capitalised and thereafter each significant word (adjective, verb, or noun) starts with a capital letter: The Grapes of Wrath, Death of a Salesman, Cat on a Hot Tin Roof, The Sound of Music, The Lord of the Rings: The Return of the King, etc. Sometimes these words are italicised to separate their title from the rest of the sentence: *The Grapes of Wrath, Death of a Salesman, Cat on a Hot Tin Roof, The Sound of Music, The Lord of the Rings: The Return of the King,* etc.

This is a convenient time to comment on the difference between *common nouns* and *proper nouns* because it relates to the issue of capitalising the first letter of a word. A noun is a thing (e.g. boy, girl, university, company, government, etc.). Where the boy, girl, university, company, government, etc. are not identified, then that noun is called a 'common noun'. Common nouns are all around us (hence the adjective, *common*). We do not grace a common noun with a capital letter because, well, they are common. Otherwise, we would end up with sentences like *The Boy and Girl played with a Ball then sat on the Fence and talked about Holidays and Cakes and Things.* However, when nouns refer to a specific person, place or thing (usually an organisation), then it is called a 'proper noun' and the first letter of a proper noun is adorned with a capital letter: Helen, the University of Glasgow, Sports Direct, etc.

Italics/bold/underline

You use *italics*/**bold**/underline to emphasise words. Underline is going out of fashion. **Bold** sometimes is too much of an emphasis, unless it appears in a heading. *Italics* is a gentle way to emphasise text. In the end, it is a matter of personal preference. Don't overdo it, though, because it can give the reader a headache. If you want to emphasise certain words, then try and avoid using quotation marks (unless, of course, you are quoting someone): use italics instead.

Clean: *Its* and *it's* mean very different things.

Clumsy: 'Its' and 'it's' mean very different things.

One other use of italics is in the naming of book titles, plays, etc.:

The Death of a Salesman by Arthur Miller

Steinbeck's *The Grapes of Wrath*

The film *Gone with the Wind*

The ellipsis (. . .)

An ellipsis is a punctuation mark made up of three dots. It can be used in two ways:

- Within a quotation, to indicate that other words form part of the passage from which you are quoting but that these missing words are not what you want to highlight:

  > ... this is definitely not my intention.
  >
  > People fail to understand my views ...
  >
  > Perhaps this is true ... but I think differently.

There is the reasonable position that there is no need for an ellipsis either at the beginning of a quotation or at the end of a quotation: just enclose the part of the quotation that you are interested in and be done with it.

- Within direct speech, to indicate a pause or a thought trailing off:

  > 'I ... I don't know,' said Robert.
  >
  > 'Let me think ...', replied Sylvia, 'No, I wasn't there.'
  >
  > Alan reflected about the option on the table: 'I wonder ...'

Spelling: British English versus American English

British English, which is really English English (as opposed to Scots English, for example), differs in some respects from American English. Many of the words used in British English originate from a dictionary created by Samuel Johnson in 1755, *A Dictionary of the English Language*. This dictionary was influenced by how Johnson thought we ought to speak and write (i.e. 'proper' English), rather than common usage. In 1828, Noah Webster took a very different approach when he created a dictionary for Americans – *An American Dictionary of the English Language* – in that he based his dictionary on common usage rather than unbending allegiance to perceived rules based on Latin. Webster was also influenced by a desire for American Independence and he wanted a separate language to go with a separate country.

Let's concentrate on differences in spelling between British English and American English, because students often mix the two together (e.g. in the one sentence using *standardise*, in the next *realize*). For consistency of appearance, you ought to stick to one spelling system and not hop from one to the other. Part of the problem is that (for non-Americans) the main word processing software packages are American and therefore the in-built dictionaries are created with American English in mind.

Words ending in -re/-er, -our/-or, -ogue/-og, -ence/-ense

In Table 1.9 are examples of some obvious differences, where there should be no confusion between British English and American English, and no excuse for using them interchangeably.

Table 1.9 Words ending in -re/-er, -our/-or, -ogue/-og, -ence/-ense: examples

Words ending in -re/-er		Words ending in -our/-or		Words ending in -ogue/-og		Words ending in -ence/-ense	
British English	American English	British English	American English	British English	American English	British English	American English
Calibre	Caliber	Behaviour	Behavior	Analogue	Analog	Defence	Defense
Fibre	Fiber	Colour	Color	Catalogue	Catalog	Offence	Offense
Litre	Liter	Neighbour	Neighbor	Monologue	Monolog	Licence/License	License
Centre	Center	Candour	Candor	Dialogue	Dialog	Pretence	Pretense
Kilometre	Kilometer	Flavour	Flavor	Epilogue	Epilog		
Theatre	Theater	Rigour	Rigor	Pedagogue	Pedagog		

Words ending in -ise/-ize

These endings commonly appear interchangeably in student essays. This is not a surprise, given that British English dictionaries now offer American English as an optional spelling (e.g. organise/organize) (see Table 1.10).

Table 1.10 Words ending in -ise/-ize: examples

British English	American English
Author**ise**	Author**ize**
Critic**ise**	Critic**ize**
Real**ise**	Real**ize**
Character**ise**	Character**ize**
Emphas**ise**	Emphas**ize**
Symbol**ise**	Symbol**ize**

Other categories

There are other categories of words where the British English spelling differs from the American English spelling, for example, marve**ll**ous/marve**l**ous (ll/l), enro**l**/enro**ll** (l/ll), man**oe**uvre/man**e**uver (oe/e), h**ae**morrhage/h**e**morrhage (ae/e), t**y**re/t**i**re (y/i), che**que**/che**ck** (que/ck), jud**ge**ment/jud**g**ment (ge/g),[2] and pro-gra**mme**/progra**m** (mme/m); as well as miscellaneous words such as grey/gray, liquorice/licorice, pyjamas/pajamas, and whisky/whiskey.

If we analyse/analyze trends in spelling (and this is not to criticise/criticize), these examples are a flavour/flavor of what is to come, with British English dictionaries and catalogues/catalogs seamlessly characterised/characterized and coloured/colored by American English, perhaps symbolising/symbolizing shifts in cultural capital. However, some would argue that, until that day comes, one should, as far as possible – with an appeal to consistency and heritage – adhere to the spelling system that predominates in the country wherein you are a student.

Writing numbers

There is no global standard on how to write numbers in essays, but there are styles of writing numbers proposed by various august bodies, e.g. the American Psychological Association (APA) and the *Chicago Manual of Style* (for American English). What follows is based on advice normally given to BBC journalists starting off in their profession (and if you can't trust the BBC, then who can you trust?), available from the BBC Academy website (https://www.bbc.co.uk/academy/en/articles/art20130702112133541 [accessed 29 March 2019]).

- Numbers 0–9 are written zero, one, two, . . ., nine:

  The three articles received less than favourable reviews.

(Headings are an exception to the rule, e.g. for your essays it is permissible to write 'Essay 2' rather than 'Essay Two', although both are acceptable.)

- The same advice is given for numbers that indicate position (i.e. ordinal numbers). For example, first, second, third, fourth, . . . ninth, 10th, 11th, etc.
- Numbers after nine to be written as numerals (10, 11, 12, etc.), though some systems stick with words until the number 100 (in which case make sure to hyphenate composite numbers e.g. 55 = fifty-five):

  That brought the total number of deaths to 14.

  More than 55 applicants failed the entrance examination.

- Million is used instead of 1,000,000; and billion is used instead of 1,000,000,000:

  There were over five million displaced people.

  Netflix had accrued debts and liabilities of $20 billion.

- Use numbers when identifying any unit of measurement:

  Distances/heights: 10km, 5 miles, 4m 2cm, 10ft 3in

  Money: £42, €12, $18

  Speed: 93mph (150km/h)

  Temperature: 30F, 15C[3, 4]

  Time: 03:25 GMT

- Weight and measures: 3,000 gallons of fuel, 35 litres of petrol (note that 'litres' – and therefore 'gallons' – is not abbreviated because the letter 'l' looks like the number '1'), 8st 4lb, 20gm of butter.
- Years: 1956, 1970s (or '70s), 12-year-old whisky. Write financial years as follows: 2016–17, not 2016–2017. Other examples: mid-1930s, the man was in his mid-20s.[5]
- Write dates using the format: day (number) month (words) year (number), i.e. separate the numbers for the day and year with the word for the month:[6]

  20 March 1956

  4 October 1978

- Centuries are written as follows:

  20th Century

  100 CE (or AD100)

  500 BCE (or 500BC)

- Never start a sentence with a number. Either write the number in words or rewrite the sentence:

  Nineteen seventy-five was a bad year for farming.

  In 1975, the farming community suffered.

- Fractions are normally spelled out but can be written as a decimal number where appropriate:

  Two-thirds of patients suffered from the bug.

  Nearly one-eighth of the working population lack a pension plan.

  The margin of error was 0.01.

Pick a system for writing numbers, whether it's one used by journalists, one recommended by the APA, one reflecting the *Chicago Manual of Style* (for American English), or one devised by your own institution, and stick to it.

Useful verbs

Verbs refer to words that describe an action or state. Students are sometimes guilty of using the same limited number of verbs over and over again in their essays:

  Figure 1 *shows* . . .

  As Table 3 *shows* . . .

  Heidegger *states* . . .

  As *stated* by Russell . . .

The words that you use in an academic essay reveal more than you think, or perhaps intend. For instance, when you state 'Stevenson confirms . . .', you are accepting the truth of what Stevenson 'confirms'; similarly, when you write 'Evans claims . . .', you are casting doubt on what Evans 'claims'. Obviously, in the course of your essay, you may start off with neutral verbs (*states, outlines, discusses*, etc.), move on to verbs that suggest doubt (*claims, confuses*, etc.), and end up using verbs to suggest agreement with an author's viewpoint (*reveals, confirms*, etc.). The important point is that the words that you use to describe something reveal your state of mind.

This section presents some useful verbs, broken down into themes, for your use (Table 1.11). The entries are not exhaustive: they are there to highlight that (1) words mean something, and (2) you have options. The present tense is given for each group of words, which can easily be changed to the past tense if you prefer (e.g. from *shows* to *shown*, *illustrates* to *illustrated*, *captures* to *captured*, etc.), beginning with useful verbs to help you refer to a Figure/Table/etc.

Table 1.11 Verbs, and when to use them

When referring to figures/tables/etc.	When neutrally stating someone's viewpoint	When casting doubt/disagreeing with someone's viewpoint
Captures	Argues	Claims
Clarifies	Asserts	Confuses
Demonstrates	Believes	Contrives
Depicts	Comments	Contorts
Displays	Concludes	Embellishes
Emphasises	Considers	Fails
Highlights	Discusses	Insists
Illustrates	Explains	Persists
Lays out	Perceives	Perpetuates
Outlines	Proposes	Panders
Presents	Reflects	Trivialises
Shows	States	Wanders

A word of warning: do not go near *proved*, not even with a barge-pole (unless you are Albert Einstein reincarnated or a returning student registered under the name Noam Chomsky). Too often students think that they have proved something. You may have provided strong evidence to suggest this or that to be the case, but claiming the final word on some topic is a tall order.

Appendix A contains a fuller list of verbs from which you can choose to write what you mean.

Summary of key points

- Paragraphs are the building blocks of university essays. Keep your paragraphs focused and coherent, starting each with a topical sentence.
- Punctuation is the glue that holds sentences together. Learn how to apply this glue.
- There are many differences in spelling between British English and American English. Be consistent.
- Sometimes numbers have to be spelled out. Pick a system for writing numbers and stick to it.
- There are verbs that you can use to show a neutral position, a favoured position, or when casting doubt. Pick the one that reflects what you want to write.

2 The language that you use: The fancy stuff

Linguistic tricks and other treats
Words that students conflate
War of words

Chapter 1 highlighted formal language issues germane to essay-writing. This chapter takes you further and discusses the fancy stuff that you can use to add a little linguistic sparkle to your essay, from simple alliteration to the use of Latin. It is also important not to say the wrong thing. Unfortunately, it is not unknown for students to confuse the meaning of closely related words, e.g. *deny* with *refute, imply* with *infer, disinterested* with *uninterested,* and so on. This chapter will explain the differences between commonly conflated words. Lastly, comment will be made on the ongoing debate taking place on the rules of Standard English.

Linguistic tricks and other treats[1]

The advice in this section is best applied *after* you have answered the essay question. Marks are primarily awarded for substance, not style, so you need to focus, in the first instance, on addressing the core task on hand: the essay question. Once you have done that, then you can look at adding linguistic tricks to good effect.

Alliteration, assonance, and consonance

If you want the reader to focus on a key point in your essay, then why not exploit techniques used by poets down the ages? *Alliteration*, the repetition of the same letter or sound of words close together, is an effective linguistic trick. Alliteration helps draw attention to particular words in a sentence. For example:

Van Gogh created a colourful palette.

In this example, there are two alliterative words: **c**reated and **c**olourful. Please note that you should not use alliteration just because you can. You should do so because you want the reader to remember (note the alliteration!) something you consider important. Also, avoid overuse of alliteration in the one sentence: it reeks of a bad nursery picture book. For example:

> Van Gogh created a colourful palette to capture the calm clouds and corn-filled countryside, with nothing more than courage, conviction, and curiosity.

If you really want to be creative, throw in for effect the odd sentence that also shows off your skills in *assonance* (repetition of vowels sounds, e.g. s**o** sl**o**w, fors**a**ken gr**a**ves, sp**u**rned **u**nder, etc.) and *consonance* (repetition of non-vowel sounds, e.g. stro**ng** swi**ng**, strea**k** of luc**k**, i**mm**ediately **m**aximised, etc.).

And another thing

Never start a sentence with *and* or *but* or *because* or *or*. (Or so some people insist.) These words are given the fancy name 'conjunctions' and their role is to join coherent parts of a sentence together:

> Mathematics is difficult **and** studied only by the foolhardy.
>
> The student wanted a break, **or** at least some nourishment.
>
> The kids needed a holiday **but** the bills were piling up.
>
> The University of Glasgow attracted so many students **because** it had such a great reputation.

The meaningful bits of a sentence are called 'clauses'. Missing out a clause at the start of a sentence grates on the teeth of traditionalists:

> Mathematics is difficult. **And** studied only by the foolhardy.
>
> The student wanted a break. **Or** at least some nourishment.
>
> The kids needed a holiday. **But** the bills were piling up.
>
> The University of Glasgow was appealing. **Because** it had such a great reputation.

But there is a counter-argument, and it is two-fold. First, other conjunctions, such as *so* and *yet*, are now freely used at the start of sentences, without any harrumphing or stamping of feet:

> **So**, where does this theory leave us?
>
> **Yet**, his theory ignores the part played by relativity.

Secondly, if used on rare occasions, and with precision, a conjunction at the start of a sentence can make a forceful point. And that's a fact as plain as the nose on your face.

Figure 2.1 Fanboys

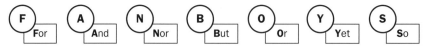

The acronym FANBOYS will help you to remember common conjunctions (Figure 2.1).

Communicates clearly

Does *clearly* come before or after *communicates*? Words that end in -ly are called adverbs and they appear beside verbs (action words). In the example *communicates clearly*, 'communicates' is from the verb 'to communicate'; and 'clearly', it is an adverb. An adverb modifies the verb. But where is it placed? *Ad* is Latin for *to*, and *verb* is from the Latin for *word*. Adverb means you add the modifying word to the verb (i.e. after the verb):

Speaks slowly [*Speaks* is the verb, *slowly* is the adverb].

Laughs heartily [*Laughs* is the verb, *heartily* is the adverb].

Eats noisily [*Eats* is the verb, *noisily* is the adverb].

However, following the verb + adverb rule is not always the best option:

He *drank quietly* his beer then left.

No one drinks quietly their beer. Much better is:

He *quietly drank* his beer then left.

Adverbs also appear at the beginning of a sentence, punctuated with a comma:

Realistically, he has no chance of winning.

Ideally, everyone should be treated equally.

Surprisingly, the party was a great success.

Fortunately, the bell rang and put everyone out of their misery.

Finally, she appeared.

Not all adverbs end in -ly. There are other words that modify verbs. For example, *almost, very, never, often, yesterday, today*, and *tomorrow*.

Dangling conversations

When we see the words *with, for, at, in, of*, and *to* in *a sentence*, we expect other words to follow:

He was *with* his wife.

It is worth fighting *for* liberty.

The train arrived *at* the station.

No one was *in* the house.

The company ran out *of* money.

The students were heading *to* Amsterdam.

Ending a sentence with *with, for, at, in, of,* or *to* is claimed to be bad English. Yet, we do this all the time when talking to each other and no one bats an eyelid. Let's look at two examples:

Who are you going with?

With whom are you going?

The first sentence, ending with 'with', is natural and clearly communicates a query. The second sentence, although clear, is stilted and unnatural. The only people to talk like that, and write like that, are those who want to be perceived as speaking and writing 'proper' English. Also, the sentence ending in a preposition (that's what these types of words are called) is so clear that there is no expectation of other words to follow.

Let's look at another two examples:

Liberty is worth fighting for.

It is worth fighting for liberty.

The first sentence is clear, punchy, starts with the thing that is worth fighting for (liberty), and ends with punchy alliteration (**f**ighting **f**or), with no expectation that other words are to come after the preposition 'for'. Its only sin is that it ends in a preposition. The alternative sentence is perfectly acceptable but lacks the oomph of the first.

What exactly is the objection about a dangling preposition? Let's revisit the examples above:

Who are you going *with*?

With whom are you going?

Liberty is worth fighting *for*.

It is worth fighting *for liberty*.

The first example separates the preposition ('with') and the subject it is related to ('whom'); the alternative line brings them together ('With whom . . .'). Similarly, the second example separates subject and preposition ('Liberty . . . for'); the fourth line brings them together ('. . . for liberty'). And that's it.

To be fair, the word 'preposition' – pre-position (*pre* meaning *before*) – indicates its purpose: to position itself before its subject (e.g. *with* his wife, *for* liberty, *at* the station, *in* the house, *of* money, *to* Amsterdam, etc.). Thus, when the eyes of some, accustomed to this union, observe a separation of preposition and subject, then this results in a sad shake of the head and a lament about standards going to the dogs. In the distant past, this positioning of words (this is called 'grammar') was taught to those of a particular status in Britain and its colonies, a tradition that was maintained with a vice-like grip until the 1960s. Some aspects of grammar have relaxed since then, but nostalgia, even when opposed with reason and common usage, is a powerful barrier to evolution.

The bottom line is this: if the preposition is left dangling, leaving a feeling of incompleteness (e.g. 'He walked ahead of'), then, of course, complete the preposition ('He walked ahead of me'); if the sentence is clear, and it's only a craving for a classist and colonial grammar that is unfulfilled, then get over it, because prepositions are not worth fighting for.

Latin for clever clogs

While substance always takes precedence over style, the occasional use of a Latin phrase can give your essay a feeling of scholarship. If over-used, however, or used artificially, it can come across as pretentious. Here is a list of useful Latin phrases followed by examples:

- *Ad hoc*: for this (particular situation).

  The company created an ad hoc committee to oversee the changes.

  The CEO had no choice but to hire staff on an ad hoc basis.

- *Ad infinitum*: to infinity (something that goes on and on).

  He talked about himself ad infinitum.

- *Annus horribilis*: horrible year.

  The year 1927 was an annus horribilis for Wall Street.

- *Annus mirabilis*: wonderful/miraculous year. Annus mirabilis can also mean a notable/pivotal year, either in terms of good or bad events.

  All the staff were invited to celebrate this annus mirabilis.

  The year 1967 was Celtic's annus mirabilis, notable for the Lisbon Lions winning the European Cup.

- *A priori*: what is before (that is, knowledge that is based on theory rather than empirical observation).

  His upbringing may well be a factor but it cannot be assumed a priori. Let's wait for the report.

  There is no a priori reason to believe that 'all men are created equal'; in fact, history proves otherwise.

Scientists have no experience of other universes, so must base their conclusions on a priori grounds.

- *Bona fide*: with good faith. Someone acting in good faith without intention to deceive. Also interpreted to mean real/genuine.

  The company made a bona fide offer to the trade union.

  She was a bona fide expert in martial arts.

- *Bona fides*: good faith.

  By paying a deposit, they demonstrated their bona fides.

- *Caveat*: warning/proviso.

  The condition of sale included a number of caveats.

  The advice given here comes with an important caveat.

  The accountant added the usual caveat to his figures.

- *Caveat emptor*: buyer beware.

  It is clear, given the troubled history of this company, that this is a case of caveat emptor.

  Caveat emptor applies when you buy from an unknown source.

- *Circa*: about/around. Used when no one knows the exact date something was done.

  It was painted circa 1830.

- *Cui bono/malo*: who gains/loses.

  The question remains: cui bono?

- *De facto*: from the fact (to describe a situation that exists, whether legally recognised or not).

  Glasgow is the de facto capital of football in Scotland.

  The Government wanted to make the next election a de facto referendum on Brexit.

  Although nothing was said, it was obvious that he was the de facto leader of the gang.

- *Et al.*: and others. *Et al.* is an abbreviation of *et alia*. Used when referencing, in the body of your essay, a publication written by three or more authors (saves writing the other author names).

  Burns *et al.* (2010) have a different perspective on elitism.

  Thomson *et al.* (2015) make obvious their distaste of capitalism.

- *Ibid.*: in the same place. *Ibid.* is an abbreviation of *ibidem*, hence the period after *ibid*. It is used to indicate that you are referring to the *previously* cited source.

> Barlow and Hogarth (2007) argue that mobile technologies are detrimental to the educational development of university students. Perceptions of the advantages of interconnectivity are often exaggerated. Even the simple skill of handwriting has been replaced by ungrammatical abbreviations (*ibid.*).

- *Inter alia*: among other things.

  > The job includes, inter alia, teaching and research.

  > The student's essay lacks, inter alia, relevance, basic writing skills, and credible references.

- *Ipso facto*: by the fact itself.

  > I was standing in the street corner and, according to some, ipso facto I was up to no good.

  > A degree, although of personal benefit, is not an ipso facto guarantee of employment.

- *Magnum opus* (or *opus magnum*): great work.

  > Marx's magnum opus, *Das Kapital*, was published in 1861.

- *Non-sequitur*: it does not follow (i.e. a conclusion that does not follow from the premise).

  > His argument is based on a non-sequitur: the fact that someone drives a fancy car does not mean that they are rich.

- *Op. cit.*: from the work cited. *Op. cit.* is an abbreviation of *opere citato*. It is used to refer to a source that you have already cited (somewhere) in your essay. *Op. cit.* is different from *ibid.* in that *ibid.* refers only to the last source cited whereas *op. cit.* refers to a source cited *somewhere* previously in your essay, i.e. it need not be the last source cited in your discussion.

  > Biggam and Murphy (2007) recommend a strategic approach to tackling plagiarism in universities. Other academics adopt a similar position (Thomson, 2003; Edwards, 2005; Smith, 2006). Differences of opinion surface, however, when it comes to deciding upon appropriate levels of punishment for transgressors. Some researchers argue for leniency, claiming that students are victims themselves. Biggam and Murphy (op. cit.) refute this line of argument.

- *Per se*: by itself, as such.

  > A smoking gun is not, per se, proof of guilt.

  > The dog's aggression, per se, is not the problem: it is the lack of control exercised by the owner.

- *Prima facie*: at first sight, on the face of it.

  > Given that the boy had the stolen apples in his pocket, there is a prima facie case that he is the culprit.

- *Quid pro quo*: something for something (else).

> The policeman and his informer operated on a quid pro quo basis
>
> The lift to work in the morning was a quid pro quo for cooking lessons in the evening.

- *Sic*: thus, so, as it stands. This was covered in Chapter 1, but is worth revisiting. *Sic* is used within a quotation to indicate that the author of the quotation has made an error, grammatical or otherwise, but that the error is not yours. It always appears in square brackets, is normally italicised, and has no full stop because it is a proper word in its own right.

> The politician apologised in writing to his constituents, claiming that he 'was trully [*sic*] sorry for what happened'.

- *Sine qua non*: a necessary condition.

> Loyalty is a sine qua non for this job.
>
> A desire to learn is a sine qua non for self-improvement.

- *V.i.*: Latin for *vide infra* and means 'see below'. Typically used when referring to diagrams, figures, etc., but can also be used to refer to previous discussion/points.

> The arguments against capitalism are numerous (*v.i.*, Table 6).
>
> As well as the disadvantages inherent in elitism (*v.i.*), there is also the matter of morality to consider.

- *Vice versa*: the other way around.

> Supply needs demand and vice versa.
>
> She loves him dearly, and vice versa.

- *V.s.*: Latin for *vide supra* and means 'see above'.

> The statistics tell a different story (*v.s.*, Figure 3.2).
>
> The history of Ireland has been one of turmoil (*v.s.*) but the future is one of optimism.

- *Viz.*: namely.

> There are two things he craves, viz.: chocolates and ice-cream.
>
> His theory has one major flaw, viz., that no one understands it.

Metaphors and similes

A *metaphor* is a description that makes a comparison that cannot be literally true but that, through colourful exaggeration, makes a point:

> She had a heart of gold.
>
> He cried crocodile tears.

The boy was a bad apple.

Her past was a closed book.

Blair promised a sea-change in political engagement.

Trade unions complained about the political power wielded by fat cats.

Low taxation was a sacred cow that Conservatives were reluctant to slay.

When a metaphor becomes worn out and tired, it loses its va-va-voom. In which case, it is better to invent your own metaphor, one that shakes a sentence back to life.

A *simile* is like a metaphor, except the comparison is made explicit through the words 'as' and 'like':

The soldier was *as* brave *as* a lion.

He sat *as* still *as* a mouse.

She came across *as* tough *as* nails.

He slept *like* a baby.

They were behaving *like* children.

The words struck him *like* a bullet through the heart.

Clichés

Clichés are well-worn phrases that are as common as muck. The word cliché is from the French verb *clicher*, meaning *to stereotype*. Examples of clichés include: *over the moon, hit the ground running, at the end of the day, take the bull by the horns, every cloud has a silver lining, the pot calling the kettle black*. Over time, metaphors and similes can also become clichés, examples of which include: *raining cats and dogs, like a lead balloon*, and *as cold as ice*. Even Shakespeare's *all the world's a stage* has had its day.

It is possible to resuscitate a cliché by altering it in a novel way. You can do this by changing the punch word to fit your specific message, thus exploiting the reader's knowledge and, at the same time, giving them a surprise. Examples include: *all the world's a cage, hit the ground screaming, read between the fines, ignorance is Chris*, and so on.

Get into the habit of including a fresh metaphor or simile in your essay. It can be effective (and fun), particularly when you create your own imagery.

Onomatopoeia

Splash! Oomph! Pow! are all examples of onomatopoeia (i.e. where the sound is the meaning). Water is not endowed with the power of speech, much less English, and so, unsurprisingly, it does not make the sound Splash! Similarly, if you have ever been punched in the face, it is highly unlikely that at the point of contact, you heard the sound Pow! Nonetheless, onomatopoeic words are words that, over time, we have come to associate with particular sounds. Some onomatopoeic words are more effective than others. For example, although sausages don't actually *sizzle*, the word is wonderfully evocative. Generally, in a university essay, avoid onomatopoeic words that come attached with an obligatory exclamation mark: it is not a comic book that you are writing. There are other onomatopoeic words that can make your essay glitter: *bubble, clatter, click, crackle, fizz, hiccup, rattle, splutter*, to tip-toe through a few.

The short paragraph

And sentence. Although the standard paragraph in a university essay contains a topic sentence, body sentences, and an optional concluding/summary sentence, that is not always the case. Conventions can be broken. Similarly, although the length of a meaningful paragraph has never been quantified, short paragraphs in a university essay suggest lack of meaning, and are therefore discouraged. However, if you want to draw attention to a key observation, based on what you have discussed, then you can insert, for effect, a short newspaper-style paragraph:

> The ramifications of adopting this policy are clear: the ethical standing of the company's reputation, built up over many years, would be in tatters overnight.

You can also breach the rules of sentence construction to draw the reader's attention to an observation. As with the short paragraph, you do so only rarely, or the effect is lost (or worse, it becomes irritating). For example: *He waited. For his chance. Then pounced.* The trick of the grammatically challenged short sentence (or inter-connected short sentences) is to write a complete sentence, then take its parts and separate them with full stops. Like this:

> I would rather stand naked, in public, gritting a rose between my teeth.

> I would rather stand. Naked. In public. Gritting a rose. Between my teeth.

The single-word sentence can also be used to good effect, particularly at the end of a paragraph, or even as the last word, literally, in your essay:

> . . . These damaging policies should be stopped. Now.

It is important to emphasise that the short paragraph, grammatically challenged sentence, and one-word sentence, should be, like a robin on your windowsill, a rare event.

To boldly go

Believe it or not, there is much angst in some quarters on whether or not Captain James T. Kirk should have sent the Starship Enterprise *to boldly go*, or *to go boldly*, 'where no man has gone before'. British English grammar is based on Latin grammar. Latin verbs (action words) always mean 'to *something*' (e.g. *amare*, to love; *pugnare*, to fight; *ambulare*, to walk). In other words, in Latin there is no other word that can come between 'to' and 'love', 'to' and 'fight', 'to' and 'walk', etc.

Those who invented British English grammar decided to replicate this practice. That is why traditional grammarians refuse to split 'to' and *something*, and insist on placing adverbs (words that usually, but not always, end in *-ly*) after 'to' and *something*. Examples include: to eat noisily, to run awkwardly, to dance merrily, etc. However, it sounds more natural to the modern ear when we go against this convention and place the adverb between the 'to' and *something*. Examples include: to awkwardly run, to merrily dance. This is called 'splitting the infinitive'. These days, no one reaches out *to shake warmly* your hand; nor do we want *to understand really* life.

If splitting an infinitive seems more natural to you, then go ahead and split that infinitive. You will not lose marks for doing so. To think differently is to foolishly maintain adherence to a linguist convention that defies common sense. Or, if you prefer, to differently think is to maintain foolishly adherence to a linguistic convention that defies common sense.

Words that students conflate[2]

Affect/effect

Affect means 'to influence or move or make a difference to', usually in the context of human behaviour and emotions:

> He was adamant that the windfall would not affect his lifestyle.
>
> She complained that the heat affected her performance.
>
> He was greatly affected by the death of his mother.
>
> She couldn't understand why a conversation with a complete stranger affected her so badly.
>
> The rain will affect their travel plans.

Effect means 'result':

> The artist experimented until he got the effect he wanted.
>
> The effect of over-eating is well known.
>
> The after-effects of partying and too much alcohol are plain to see.

Effect can also be used to mean 'bring about', as in *politicians sometimes effect policies that benefit society.*

If you substitute *change(d)* or *influence(d)* for 'affect(ed)', and *result(ed)* for 'effect(ed)', then you shouldn't go wrong.

Among/between

Between refers to two things that are separated:

The house sits between a farm and a factory.

Jason sat between John and Leanne.

Among refers to something in a group of things:

The escaped prisoner hid among the crowd.

She swam among the dolphins, angel fish, and turtles.

Around/round

Around means *about* (e.g. 'He's around here somewhere'), whereas *round* suggests circularity (e.g. 'Kay cycled round Mont Blanc'). However, over time, the words have become close to synonymous, which means that you can usually use them interchangeably (e.g. 'We drove around the block', 'We drove round the block'). Be aware, though, that there are occasions when you might want to select one over the other, e.g. 'He was around at the time of the Crusades' means he was 'about/alive at the time of the Crusades'; whereas, 'He was round at the time of the Crusades', might be construed as an adverse comment on someone's figure.

Criterion/criteria

Criterion refers to a standard or condition (singular) whereas *criteria* refers to standards or conditions (plural):

There was only one criterion for entry to the party: you had to bring your own booze.

Applicants had to meet the following criteria: hold a current driving license, have experience of sales, and speak French fluently.

Deny/refute

To *deny* something is to refuse to agree that something is true. It can also mean to refuse (someone) something:

He denied that he was the one who stole the cake.

The farmer denied hikers access to his field.

Refute is stronger than deny. Refute means to prove something is wrong:

> He refuted the claim that he was always late for work.

Disinterested/uninterested

Disinterested means neutral, unbiased. *Uninterested* means someone who is bored or couldn't care less:

> The chairperson adopted a disinterested stance throughout the meeting.
>
> The child was uninterested in watching the news.

Farther/further

There is no difference in meaning between the two words. Stick with further. Farther is an old-fashioned word that is rarely used. Besides, no one says *we can go no farther*.

Essentially, there is no difference between 'farther' and 'further' but there is a tendency to use 'farther' for physical distances and 'further' for figurative/metaphorical distances:

> We travelled farther today.
>
> What is the farthest point from here?
>
> Alan and Anne stayed a further week at the villa.
>
> The witness had nothing further to add.
>
> The group departed without further delay.
>
> He had gone furthest in academia than anyone in his family.

Using *further* in all of these examples would not present a problem. 'Farther' should be the farthest thing from your mind: stick to using 'further' in all cases.

Fewer/less

Fewer people couldn't care less about this. *Fewer* is used when referring to people or things that can be counted:

> Right: Fewer people attend church than ever before.
>
> Wrong: Less people attend church than ever before.
>
> Right: The club had fewer than ten members.
>
> Wrong: The club had less than ten members.
>
> Right: The team conceded fewer fouls than the opposition.
>
> Wrong: The team conceded less fouls than the opposition.

Less is used for something that cannot be counted or has no plural:

> He had less time than he thought.
>
> As each day passed, he reflected less and less about his past.
>
> The job paid less money than his old job.

Less is also used in measurements of time, distance, and weight:

> The relationship lasted less than one month.
>
> The soldier had less than two miles to go.
>
> The newborn baby weighed less than 5 pounds.

Imply/infer

To *imply* something is to suggest, or hint at, something. Something not clearly stated:

> The report implied that we should prepare for organisational change.
>
> The speaker said that he did not mean to imply that women were inferior to men.

Infer is the opposite of *imply*. To infer is to come to a clearly stated conclusion based on evidence:

> One could infer from the policy document that tackling cybercrime was not a priority.
>
> The sudden surge of fans outside led the press to infer that the celebrity had arrived.

Incredible

Incredible is derived from the Latin word *incredibilis*, meaning not believable (in-)believable (*credibilis* or credible). That has been diluted to include something that is hard to believe:

> It is incredible that Hitler was allowed to rise to power.
>
> Incredible as it seems, slavery still exists today.

Common usage largely interprets 'incredible' to mean something extraordinary:

> The sight before him was incredible.
>
> He had an incredible tale to tell.

Informally, 'incredible' is used in everyday speech to mean something that is wonderful:

> He scored an incredible goal.
>
> She was an incredible woman.
>
> The manager praised everyone for their incredible effort over this difficult period.

Incredibly, 'incredible' is also used as an adverb to mean 'really, really':

> The teacher was incredibly patient with the children.
>
> He was incredibly stupid.
>
> The film was incredibly sad.

In academic writing, avoid using incredible to mean 'wonderful' or 'really, really'. It's incredibly irritating.

It's/its

It's is shorthand for *it is* (or *it has*). If you don't know the meaning of *its* by now, it's probably because you haven't read Chapter 1.

Literally

Literally means 'in actual fact'. So, statements such as *he is literally on a different planet* are nonsense (unless he is on a different planet).

Number of/amount of

Number of refers to something that can be counted (hence number of); *amount of* refers to things that we can't count:

> The number of people asking for tickets exceeded supply.
>
> The solicitor raised a number of objections.
>
> The amount of effort required to meet the financial goal was praised by the manager.
>
> The amount of time required to perform the task acted as a disincentive.

Practice/practise

Practice with a 'c' is a noun, i.e. a thing. It usually refers to a profession, a common procedure, or a repeated skill or time spent on an activity:

> The new dental practice already had a waiting list.
>
> She joined the medical practice to help people.

The manager introduced an ethical code of practice.

No really knew how the policies would work in practice.

It is common practice to let students choose their own dissertation topic.

It was obvious to everyone that the boxer needed more sparring practice.

Practise with an 's' is a verb, i.e. an action word. It is something that you do:

I love to practise at the piano.

I practise French every day.

They were practising for the competition.

She was a practising lawyer.

In American English, both the noun and the verb are spelled *practice*.

That/which

In British English, you can generally use *that* and *which* interchangeably:

The language that we use.

The language which we use.

However, *which* is useful when you wish to add additional information about something:

We arrived at the party, which was heaving with people.

She entered the cafe, which was empty.

He offered his hand, which I accepted.

Note that when you use *which* to indicate additional information, you need to precede that additional information with a comma, otherwise the meaning of the sentence will change. For example, *We arrived at the party which was heaving with people* suggests that there were other parties but that you choose to arrive at the one that was heaving with people; whereas *We arrived at the party, which was heaving with people*, merely highlights a feature of the party that you attended.

Their/there/they're

Their refers to ownership of something:

Their *coats* were ragged.

Their *views* on slavery were obnoxious.

There refers to a place:

> You will find the treasure over there.
>
> You live in Toulouse? I went there for my holidays!

There is also used in 'there is' and 'there are':

> There is no such thing as a ghost.
>
> There are only so many ways to skin a cat.

Finally, *there* can be used to comfort someone (usually accompanied by gentle caressing):

> There, there.

They're is a contraction of 'they are'. You should not be using contractions in university essays.

These/those

These is the plural of *this*, and *those* is the plural of *that*. *This* is used when referring to something near, *that* when referring to something further away. Similarly, *these* is used when referring to something near, *those* when referring to something further away. So, *this* and *these* for things close at hand, *that* and *those* for things not close at hand:

> 'I cherish this medal,' said William, holding it aloft for all to see.
>
> That hill over there will be difficult to climb.
>
> These paintings are beautiful.
>
> Those ships are specks on the horizon.
>
> This house is lovely, but these carpets have to go!
>
> That dog bit me, and those people just stood and watched.
>
> This dog [beside you] bit me, and these people [beside you] just stood and watched.

Unconscious/subconscious

When you are *unconscious*, you are knocked out. In such a state, the only thing you will be doing *unconsciously* is dreaming. If you write 'most purchasing decisions are made unconsciously', then you are in danger of conjuring up an image of zombies staggering around a shop.

Subconscious means the things that influence your behaviour are *below* your conscious awareness, i.e. you are not overtly aware of them. Thus, 'most purchasing decisions are made subconsciously' cannot be conflated with the living dead staring unblinkingly at supermarket shelves.[3]

Given these issues, it's better to play safe, knock *unconscious* on the head, and use *subconscious* instead; unless, that is, you really are talking about things that people don't want to talk about; or you have a thing for zombies.

Were/where/we're

Were is the plural of *was*, referring to a collective in the past tense:

> They were tired but perked up at the sight of food.
>
> They were intent on walking further but blisters soon put a stop to that plan.

Were is also used when considering hypothetical or imagined situations. This is called the *subjunctive*:

> If he were taller, he could reach that shelf.
>
> If I were a billionaire, I would buy a yacht.
>
> If they were superheroes, then they could save the world.

If what is being considered might be true, then *was* is used instead of *were*:

> If he was afraid, he didn't mention it.
>
> If I was the person who bumped into you, then I apologise.

Where refers to a place:

> Where are you?
>
> Where did I put my glasses?

We're is a contraction of 'we are'. Not to be used in university essays.

Who/whom

The bell tolls for *whom*. 'To *whom* it may concern.' If you find yourself strangely attracted to *whom*, then here's how to avoid conflating your *whos* with your *whoms*. Most sentences have a subject, verb, and an object (Table 2.1). In other

Table 2.1 Subject, verb, and object

Subject	Verb	Object
Who	loves	you?
You	love	whom?

words, who is doing what to whom. For example, in the sentence 'I love you', the subject is *I*, the verb is *love*, and the object is *you*. If we were to use *who*, and then *whom*, in the sentence 'I love you', then *who* becomes the subject, *whom* the object.

If you are still unsure, then if you can substitute he/she in the sentence for *who*, then *who* is correct; if you can substitute him/her in the sentence for *whom*, then *whom* is correct. The key thing to remember is that *who* is used when it is the subject of the verb; *whom*, when it is the object of the verb. Let's look at some examples:

Subject

Who is the manager? (*Who* is the subject of *is*.)

Her boyfriend, *who* loved to ski, died in an avalanche. (*Who* is the subject of *loved*.)

Object

The teacher expelled *whom*? (*Whom* is the object of *expelled*.)

With *whom* did you speak? (*Whom* is the object of the preposition *with*.)

Prepositions

This brings us on to prepositions. A preposition is usually a small word that helps connect parts of a sentence. Common prepositions are *to*, *by*, *with*, *for*, and *from*. When prepositions occur at the start of a sentence, then *whom* is used:

From whom did you receive the letter?

To whom was the letter sent?

Whom is rarely used in speech, and it is becoming increasingly less common in writing too. There is only one situation where it is compulsory to use *whom*, and that is when *quantifiers* appear in front of *whom*. Quantifies are words that indicate the quantity of something:

The children listened attentively, *all of whom* were eager to learn.

The brothers waited outside the headmaster's office, *both of whom* knew what was coming.

The men were nervous, *few of whom* had fought in a war.

The players were exhausted, *several of whom* had already received treatment for cramp.

The students were silent, *most of whom* were bored stiff.

The policemen formed a line, *many of whom* carried batons and shields.

Incidentally, between *you and me*, which one of the following is correct?

> John took Jason and I to the museum.
>
> John took Jason and me to the museum.

Before we (meaning the royal 'we') provide the answer, let's consider a simpler version:

> John took I to the museum.
>
> John took me to the museum.

The correct version is obviously *John took me to the museum*, which means that the correct version for *John took Jason and I/me to the museum* is likewise *John took Jason and me to the museum*, because it doesn't matter who else John took – he also took me. You have just learned a trick on how to differentiate between *I* and *me* when a number of things happen to two or more people: *me* is used instead of *I* (Table 2.2).

Technically, it is the verb (the action word) in a sentence that determines whether to use *me* or *I*. If the verb is acting on you, then it's *me* that is used. In each of the sentences in Table 2.3, the verbs 'chased', 'sent', 'shared', and 'watched'

Table 2.2 Correct use of *me*

I or me?	Correct version
The dog chased Robert and I/me.	The dog chased Robert and me.
The email was sent to Eileen, Joseph, and I/me.	The email was sent to Eileen, Joseph, and me.
The cake was shared between Brad and I/me.	The cake was shared between Brad and me.
The film was watched by Paul, Bob, and I/me.	The film was watched by Paul, Bob, and me.

Table 2.3 Correct use of *I*

I or me?	Correct version
Robert and I/me were chased by the dog.	Robert and I were chased by the dog.
Eileen, Joseph, and I/me were sent an email.	Eileen, Joseph, and I were sent an email.
Brad and I/me shared the cake.	Brad and I shared the cake.
Paul, Bob, and I/me watched the film.	Paul, Bob, and I watched the film.

all act on 'you' (the dog chased you, the email was sent to you, the cake was shared with you, the film was watched by you), so *me* is the correct usage.

If the verb in a sentence acted on something else, and not you, then *I* would be the correct usage. In each of these sentences, the verb is acting on something else, and not you: 'chased by the dog', 'sent an email', 'shared the cake', and 'watched the film'. In other words, if the verb is referring to something else and not you, then *I* is the correct usage.

Let's look at another example:

Alan and I sat on the sofa.

Alan and me sat on the sofa.

Which is the correct version? First of all, identify the verb. It is 'sat'. It refers to the sofa ('sat on the sofa'). So, *I* is used, and the correct version is *Alan and I sat on the sofa.*

Another example:

Who is coming to the cinema with Sandra and I?

Who is coming to the cinema with Sandra and me?

The verb is 'coming' and it refers 'to the cinema', not you. Therefore, the correct version is *Who is coming to the cinema with Sandra and I?*

In summary, *me* is used when the verb is acting on *you* (e.g. 'The party started without Karl and me'), and *I* is used when it is not (e.g. 'Steven and I went to the party').

War of words

The way that we use words when we write in formal situations (e.g. essays, newspaper articles, reports, etc.) has caused much debate, and even outright hostility, between two groups of protagonists: traditional grammarians and cultural linguists. The former insist that sentence structure must adhere to strict rules; the latter state that the rules of formal written language ought to evolve with the times.

The problem can be placed squarely at the conquering feet of the Romans. They may have given us roads and baths but, unfortunately, for spite, they also gave us grammar. British English grammar is based on Latin grammar, a wheeze thought up by those who wanted to create a standard in written English, appropriately referred to as Standard English. There was one major flaw in this seminal decision: English is not Latin. The language, including grammar, that we use in conversation appears natural to us because it is regional, informal, changes with the times, and is something we practise every day, unlike formal written English with its slavish obedience to something that was created a long time ago. This perhaps explains why many of us struggled to write 'proper' English at school.

The cultural linguists do not disagree that there should be rules about Standard English, only that the rules should not be fossilised and resistant to change. Traditional grammarians disagree, and that is why they favour sentences like *To go boldly* over *To boldly go*; *It is worth fighting for liberty* over *Liberty is worth fighting for*; *With whom are you going?* over *Who are you going with?*; and *Alan and I watched a film* over *Me and Alan watched a film.*[4]

Don't despair. It is rare that those marking your essays will throw you in the dungeon if you split your infinitives (damn those Romans), provocatively dangle your prepositions, or turn your back on whomever you wish.

Summary of key points

- Learn the tricks of writing, from alliteration, to useful Latin terms, to exploiting metaphors and similes, to the occasional short paragraph and even shorter sentence.
- Understand the words that students often get wrong, and you won't go wrong.
- There is a debate about the rules of Standard English. Don't be a martyr: wait until you have completed your essay(s) before you rebel.

3 Give credit where credit is due

He said, she said (in-text referencing)
Recording your sources (the reference list)

Plagiarism is where you take credit for someone else's work, in whole or in part, and claim it as your own. In the context of university essay-writing, it is academic theft and fraud wrapped up as honest endeavour. Don't do it: it is unethical, easy to spot, punishable, and not worth the effort. Referencing is the antidote to plagiarism. It is also an important criterion upon which the scholarship of a university essay is judged: an absence of references, or inadequate/poor referencing, and any hope of a meritorious submission will be seriously holed. This chapter teaches you how to cite sources in the body of your essay and how to create a reference list at the end of your essay. In other words, it will guide you through giving credit where credit is due, and securing top marks for referencing in the process.[1]

He said, she said (in-text referencing)

Referencing in the body of your essay is called *in-text* referencing. You reference for a number of reasons: to provide evidence that you are knowledgeable in your subject area; to back up your points; to acknowledge your sources; to allow others to see who or what influenced your thinking (and so make a judgement on whether or not you have correctly interpreted those sources); to present a scholarly sheen to your essay; and, of course, because you get marks for doing so.

The sources that you cite should be *recent, relevant,* and *reliable* (see Figure 3.1). Let's look at the first of these 3 Rs: *recent.* If your references are out of date, then your essay is out of date. For example, if you are discussing current e-security issues and your most recent reference is for 2010, then your essay is out of date. Be careful though, not all credible sources need to be recent. For instance, you may wish to provide some historical background information;

Figure 3.1 The 3 Rs of referencing

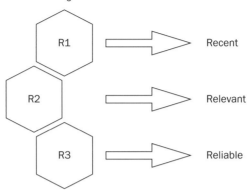

R1   ⟹   Recent

R2   ⟹   Relevant

R3   ⟹   Reliable

you may be using theories posited by Marx (either Karl or Groucho); you may be discussing the work of Michelangelo; or, you may be discussing seminal theories or ideas in your field (e.g. Freud in a psychology essay). Nevertheless, regardless of the topic, there will be modern academic voices offering a view. In the context of referencing, part of your task is to cite these contemporary sources (to show that you are well-read and that you have your finger on the pulse of academic opinion).

The criteria *relevant* and *reliable* is non-negotiable. A source that is *relevant* is one that relates to the point you are making in your essay, whether it relates to background information, an explanation, or a voice in support of, or against, a stated position, or even, for some light-hearted relief, a witty observation. Padding your essay with irrelevant sources serves no useful purpose. *Reliable* sources are more likely to be found in peer-reviewed publications, such as journals, conference proceedings, and academic books. These can be acquired through university libraries and database portals. That is not to say that you can't use material found on the internet: if it's useful and informed or evidence-based, then use it. However, do so sparingly. You are writing an academic essay, so the bulk of your references ought to come from bona fide academic sources.

Let's get down to the nitty-gritty of referencing. There are a number of *styles* of referencing. This book adopts the Harvard style, often referred to as the author–date style (for reasons that will become clear). Different styles have traditionally been favoured by different disciplines (see Table 3.1), but Harvard is easy to use and is multi-disciplinary, hence its popularity.

So, how do you cite sources in the body of your essay? There are two ways you can cite sources: indirectly and directly.

Let's start with *indirect* referencing because it is the easiest to do and the most common. This is where you make a point and cite your source in round brackets (commonly referred to as parentheses). Here is an example using Harvard referencing:

The banking crisis of 2008 led to a breach of trust in the science of economics (Rodgers, 2016).

Table 3.1   Referencing styles

Referencing style	Typical usage
APA (American Psychological Association)	Social Sciences (Economics, Political science, Geography, Sociology, etc.)
Chicago	English language, History and Fine Arts
Harvard	A generic style used across most discipline areas
IEEE (Institute of Electrical and Electronics Engineers)	Computer Science & Electronics
MHRA (Modern Humanities Research Association)	Humanities (Languages, Literature, History, Philosophy, Religion, the Arts, etc.)
MLA (Modern Language Association)	Humanities (Languages, literature, History, Philosophy, Religion, the Arts, etc.)
OSCOLA	Law
Vancouver	Medicine and Science

Source: Biggam, J. (2018) *Succeeding with Your Master's Dissertation*. 4th edn. London: Open University Press.

With indirect referencing, you are stating that the source in brackets expressed the same view in a particular year, in a particular source (book, newspaper, etc. – the precise details of which you will provide in a reference list). Within the brackets, you provide two pieces of information: the author's surname and year of publication, separated by a comma. It's easy to see why the label *author–date* system has been attached to the Harvard style of referencing.

If there are two (or more) authors that expressed the same view, then you would place them in chronological order, separated by a semi-colon:

> The banking crisis of 2008 led to a breach of trust in the science of economics (Rodgers, 2016; Edgar, 2018).

> The banking crisis of 2008 led to a breach of trust in the science of economics (Withers, 2015; Rodgers, 2016; Edgar, 2018).

Let's now deal with *direct* referencing. This is where you openly name the author in the sentence. Once again, you still need to provide two pieces of information: author and date of publication:

> Withers (2015) was clear that the banking crisis led to a breach of trust in the science of economics.

> Boulder (2018) vehemently objected to closer European integration.

> Cranston (2017) complained about a democratic deficit in universities.

With direct referencing, you now have the option to quote your source. A word of warning: do not overuse quotations. Too many quotations and your own voice will be smothered. Your marker wants to hear what you have to say: other voices are there to support your position, not the other way round. A quotation should be the icing on the cake. If quotations become an overused ingredient in your essay, then the reader will quickly get sick of them.

If a quotation is short, then embed it naturally into your sentence:

> Smith (2018, p.3) complained that 'politics is now for the few, not the many'.

> Pearson (2013, p.22) echoes this view when he states that 'time is a meaningless concept'.

> Holden (2015, p.14) expressed an unequivocal position on capital punishment when he wrote 'I abhor all forms of capital punishment'.

> 'Parliament is democracy inaction' (Reed, 2019, p.56).

Notice that when you quote a source, you must also provide a third piece of information: the page number of the publication in which the quotation can be found.

If your quotation is three or more lines in length, then you can give it a paragraph to itself. If you do so, it is normal practice to italicise the quotation and indent the paragraph (to let the reader know that it is a special paragraph, one made up of a quotation). In which case, there is no need to enclose the large quotation with quotation marks to indicate it is a quotation – the italicised (and indented) paragraph does that job:

> Saunders (2017, p.8) offers an interesting observation on 'deviant' football fan behaviour:

> > *Fans' behaviour is being misrepresented. They are not being offensive for the sake of it. They are not errant youngsters lacking in respect. They are not neds. They are the conscience of an age. The pyrotechnics and songs are an attempt to reclaim their individuality, their historical identity, their right to assert their politics. In days gone by they would be lauded as working-class heroes. Instead, they are demonised. Changed days indeed.*

When you embed a brief quotation in a sentence, it forms a natural part of the sentence, and so requires little in the way of explanation. The same cannot be said for a long quotation. A long quotation requires explanation and comment on your part. You obviously consider that the long quotation merits attention, otherwise you would not have reproduced it, so you ought to interpret the quotation for the reader and give your views on the content (e.g. do you agree/disagree with the author's view?). Long quotations, though, should be a rarity: they eat into your word count and so leave less room for you to express your own views.

There may be occasions when you are citing a source, not in the original document, but through some other source. For example, suppose that you are reading an article by Brown published in 2018 and that Brown cites Cunningham who, in turn, wrote something in 1972. If you also want to cite Cunningham, but have not read Cunningham's 1972 publication, then you have to let the reader know that you read about Cunningham in Brown's article. Example:

> Cunningham (1972, cited in Brown, 2018) predicted the demise of the shipbuilding industry in Scotland.

What if you want to cite a book title – novel, play, collection of poems, etc. – as well as an author, how do you do that in-text? Book titles are italicised. The year of publication is also required but need not be placed in brackets:

> *The Grapes of Wrath*, published in 1939, is an exceptional novel by Steinbeck.

> Beckett's *Waiting for Godot* is still as relevant today as it was when first published in 1952.

> *Selected Poems*, edited by Ted Hughes and published in 2002, is a comprehensive collection of Sylvia Plath's mature poems.

If referring to a performance – in a film, play, musical piece, etc. – then, once again, you should highlight the title in italics. In each case, you should also identify the director:

> *The Sound of Music*, directed by Robert Wise (1965), is technically similar to *West Side Story*.

> Gregory Doran's 2008 production of *Hamlet* cast David Tennant in the starring role.

> Keith Warner's 2018 interpretation of Wagner's *Der Ring des Nibelungen* is stunning in many respects.

If referring to an art work – painting, sculpture, etc. – the title of the work is italicised. The artist is also identified. If the year of creation is not known, then use the abbreviation n.d. (no date); if the year of creation is roughly known, then use the Latin term circa, or c., meaning *about*:

> *Guernica* (1937) is Picasso's most influential painting.

> E. E. Cummings' *Stripper #5* (n.d.) is an oil painting on cardboard.

> The smile in Leonard da Vinci's *Mona Lisa* (c. 1503) is a masterpiece of ambiguity.

> Michelangelo's *David* (c. 1501–1504) was created from a damaged slab of stone.

Lastly, when citing computer software, you give the title of the software, the company behind it, and the year of release. For consistency, you can italicise the title of the software, but in practice that is rarely seen (probably because the title is obvious to customers). The version of the software may also form part of the title:

> AVG anti-virus software (AVG Technologies, 2017) claims to provide fully loaded protection.

> Civilization VI (Firaxis, 2016) is the latest version of a game that has maintained a loyal following since its inception in 1999.

> Newton, an android app by Cloudburst (2016), allows users to access all their email addresses through one point of contact.

In summary, when using the Harvard system, two core pieces of information are always required when citing sources in-text: the author (i.e. creator) and date (of creation). When discussing a particular work – a book, play, film, piece of music, painting, or software application – the title is also required.

Recording your sources (the reference list)

You need to record all the sources cited in your essay for others to see. You do so via a *reference list* at the end of your essay. A reference list is a collection of all the sources – articles, books, websites, etc. – explicitly referred to in your essay. For every source that you cite in-text, you need a corresponding entry in your reference list. You could create a *bibliography* instead. The difference between a reference list and a bibliography is that the former contains a list of all the sources used in your essay, while the latter, in addition, includes other sources that you have read but not used. The advantage of a reference list is that there is a one-to-one relationship between the sources cited in your essay and the entries in your reference list. It is also clear, by looking at the reference list, which sources directly influenced your submission. The advantage of a bibliography is that it reveals all the works you read for your essay; the disadvantage, from a marker's point of view, is that it is not possible to determine, in the absence of any commentary, the relevance of the additional sources. Where the discussed sources are few but the bibliography is lengthy, there may also be the suspicion that the student has engaged in compensatory padding. This book focuses on creating a reference list, although the same approach can be applied for a bibliography.

When a marker looks at your reference list (or bibliography, if that is your choice), they do so with the following questions in mind: (1) are the references reasonably recent?; (2) are they relevant?; (3) are they reliable?; (4) are there enough references?; and (5) have they been formatted in line with academic standards?

Let's deal with points (1)–(3) first (the 3 Rs: recent, relevant, and reliable, seen in Figure 3.1). Collectively, they amount to the credibility of your sources.

A common mistake by students is to rely heavily on internet sources. When markers see too many unregulated websites in a reference list, their heart sinks. Academic credibility is achieved by largely sticking to scholarly books and articles, usually found in the university library or accessed through university databases. Table 3.2 highlights common databases that most university systems can access. JSTOR (http://www.jstor.org), which is short for **J**ournal **STOR**age, is a US-based multi-disciplinary database that includes scholarly books as well as articles and primary sources used by many universities across the globe.

Now to point (4), the question of quantity. Students are forever asking 'How many references do I need?'. There is no algorithm that will calculate the number of references you require for any given essay. Academics might reasonably respond: *use the number that you need to complete your essay*. However, that still does not help you answer your query; besides, try arguing with your marker that you only require one source of information. In reality, you do not have the opportunity to defend the length of your reference list – at least not before your essay is marked – which brings us back to the question of quantity. One could adopt a pragmatic approach based on the psychology of numbers, as whimsically captured in the following ditty:

How Many You Ask?

1 to 5 is too few, announcing to all and sundry you don't have a clue;

6 to 10 might do the trick, with one eye on basic arithmetic;

11 to 15 is a sure-fire hit, letting the world know: you're no lazy git;

16 to 20 plants your feet, firmly and squarely, amongst the elite;

anything else is just showing off; but then again, you're now a toff!

A reference list is not included in the word count. Nonetheless, some students might baulk at trying to find 11+ references for a university essay (if that is the number you deemed necessary). Actually, it's very easy to accommodate 11+ references. Consider the following sentence:

Many educationists object to elitism (Wright, 2006; Tomlinson, 2009; Heart, 2014; Reid, 2017).

The sentence cites four sources. That's four entries in a reference list. It doesn't take long at all to build up an impressive reference list. If you are serious about showing that you are well-read in the subject under discussion and that your essay is evidence-based, you will naturally gravitate towards a well-stocked reference list, particularly when you take on board your module's core and recommended reading, the texts highlighted in lecture and seminar notes, the articles that you acquire, and the authors that other authors refer to in the articles that you acquire. In short, if you are having to ask yourself the question 'Do I have enough references?', then generally you do not.

Table 3.2   Common external databases

Subject	Common external databases
Arts & Humanities	Art & Architecture Complete (EBSCO), ARTbibliograpies Modern (ProQuest), Arts & Humanities Citation Index, British Humanities Index (ProQuest), Humanities Abstracts (EBSCO), MLA International Bibliography, Social Services Abstracts, SocINDEX and ASSIA
Business & Economics	Business Source Complete (EBSCO), Emerald, FAME, Economist Historical Archive, KeyNote, Materials Business File, Mintel Reports and Osiris
Education	ERIC, Australian Education Index (ProQuest), British Education Index (ProQuest) and Teacher Reference Centre (EBSCO)
Environment	Environment Abstracts (ProQuest), Environment Engineering Abstracts, Environment Impact Statements and Pollution Abstracts
Human Resources	Croner-i Human Resources
Law	CANS Advice Notes, Lawtel, LexisLibrary, HeinOnline, HUDOC, Max Planck Encyclopedia of Public International Law and Oxford Scholarship Online (Law)
Medicine & Health Care	Cochrane Library, MEDLINE, PubMed, EMBASE: Excerpta Medica, Scopus, CINAHL, PsycINFO, Web of Knowledge, Amadeo, Clinical Trials (US National Institute of Health), NICE, ScienceDirect and Social Care Online
Multi-disciplinary	JSTOR, JISC, ZETOC and Web of Knowledge
Science & Engineering	BioMed Central, Chemical Database Service, ScienceDirect, Science Citation Index, SciFinder, Scitation, Scopus, MathSciNet, Web of Science, ACM Digital Library, Cern Document Server, Inspec, SPIRES-HEP, ACM Digital Library, Computer and Information Systems Abstracts (ProQuest), IEEE Electronic Library, Compendex, Engineering Research Database, Engineered Materials Abstracts and Environment Engineering Abstracts

Source: Biggam, J. (2018) *Succeeding with Your Master's Dissertation*. 4th edn. London: Open University Press.

Setting aside the content of your essay for the moment (discussed in detail in Chapter 4), your essay also has to look the part. Cursory first impressions, however unfair, are important in life; and university essays are not immune from that age-old truth that first impressions matter. While a 'reference list' containing only two entries might struggle to meet the Trade Descriptions Act, one with, say, 12 sources, confidently declares 'this essay is supported by 12 sources of information'. Common sense dictates which one will make the better impression.

Most markers will have a quick look at your essay (number of pages, structure, and reference list) before getting down to the nitty-gritty of detailed reading and marking, just to get a feel for your submission. A shrunken reference list will set alarm bells ringing, but a well-stocked reference list will immediately give your essay the look and feel of an academic submission.

Now, point (5): formatting your reference list. There is more to a reference list than size. Universities expect references to be formatted according to certain academic standards and provide clear guidance on what they expect in terms of formatting standards. Most universities will have general referencing advice on their website but check your student handbook, or ask a tutor, for your department's referencing guidelines. Reference formatting is a basic skill demanded of university students. Poor reference formatting will hinder any ambition to achieve a high mark. Done properly, it gives your work a professional sheen and shows your marker that you take pride in properly recording your source details. Here is what a reference list can start to look like:

References

Alstyne, V., Brynjolfsson, E. and Madnick, S. (1995) 'Why not one big database? Principles of data ownership', *Decision Support Systems*, 15, pp. 267–284.

Anderson, L. W. and Krathwohl, D. R. (2001) *A taxonomy for learning, teaching and assessment: A revision of Bloom's taxonomy of educational objectives*. New York: Longman.

Azouzi, R., Beauregard, R. and D'Amours, S. (2009) 'Exploratory case studies on manufacturing agility in the furniture industry', *Management Research News*, 32(5), pp. 424–439.

Barrett, E. and Bolt, B. (2010) *Practice as research: Approaches to creative arts enquiry*. London: Routledge.

Bates, A. (2000) *Managing technological change: Strategies for colleges and university leaders*. San Francisco, CA: Jossey-Bass.

Bell, J. and Waters, S. (2018) *Doing your research project: A guide for first-time researchers*. 7th edn. London: Open University Press.

Under the Harvard system, references are listed alphabetically. Thereafter, the details of each source are given, starting with author(s) and date of publication, followed by publication details, including the title of the publication. There is a purpose to formatting references (other than looking good and pleasing your marker). Sources need to be identified in a consistent way that is universally accepted in academia. Doing so makes it easier for academics in the same field to write to each other about their sources. The alternative – to allow academics to create their own personal referencing system – would make it difficult for the academic community to share research in an intelligible way. A referencing standard, such as Harvard or the APA, is, in effect, an open-sourced code that is there to facilitate communication but that will only work if its users understand and abide by the rules. For example, every academic would recognise the following source as a book:

> Barrett, E. and Bolt, B. (2010) *Practice as research: Approaches to creative arts enquiry*. London: Routledge.

It is the formatting – the order and punctuation of the information – that reveals the nature of the source. Of course, a more obvious way to identify the source is as follows:

> **This is a book by** Barrett, E. and Bolt, B. **It was published in** 2010. **The title is:** *Practice as research: Approaches to creative arts enquiry*. **It was published in** London **by the publisher** Routledge.

Academics would also readily identify the following source as a journal article:

> Azouzi, R., Beauregard, R. and D'Amours, S. (2009) 'Exploratory case studies on manufacturing agility in the furniture industry', *Management Research News*, 32(5), pp. 424–439.

Once again, one could easily replace it with a more expansive and explanatory version:

> **This is a journal article by** Azouzi, R., Beauregard, R. and D'Amours, S. **It was published in** 2009. **The title is:** 'Exploratory case studies on manufacturing agility in the furniture industry'. **It appeared in the journal** *Management Research News*, **in volume** 32, **in issue** 5, **and can be found between pages** 424 **and** 439 **inclusive**.

However, these additional words, although helpful to the novice, are redundant because the formatting (that is, order and punctuation of information) does the same job but using less words.

As raised earlier, different academic disciplines have favoured different styles of formatting for references (see Table 3.1). Even within the different referencing styles, there are, unfortunately, variations from one institution to another. To illustrate this point, imagine that you have a printed book in front of you and its source details are as follows:

> **Author:** Tierney, J.
>
> **Title:** Criminology

Year published: 2009

Publisher: Longman

Place of publication: London

To cite the source in-text is pretty standard from university to university:

Tierney (2009) highlights the legal words and themes required to succeed in the world of criminology.

However, recording the source information for Tierney's book in a reference list can differ slightly depending on where you seek advice. Table 3.3 shows you how Tierney's book would be recorded at the end of your essay if you were using Harvard at either the Open University or Anglia Ruskin University, sought advice from the referencing site Cite This for Me (previously called RefME), or read the book *Cite Them Right* by Pears and Shields (2019).

None of the referencing formats in Table 3.3 are wrong, even though no two are completely identical. (Can you spot the differences?) Most have the author's initial ending with a period, one doesn't; most have the year of publication enclosed within brackets, one doesn't; two have a period before the book title, two don't; all have the book title *italicised*; three have a period after the book title, one has a comma; three separate the place of publication and the publisher with a colon, one has a comma.

This lack of a common approach to creating a reference list using Harvard is reflected in the application of other referencing systems throughout academia.

Table 3.3 Referencing a book using Harvard style: different advice, different formats

Institution	Book reference
Open University (http://www.open.ac.uk/libraryservices/documents/Harvard_citation_hlp.pdf)	Tierney, J. (2009) *Criminology,* London, Longman.
Anglia Ruskin University (http://libweb.anglia.ac.uk/referencing/harvard.htm)	Tierney, J., 2009. *Criminology.* London: Longman.
Cite This for Me (http://www.citethisforme.com/guides/harvard/how-to-cite-a-book)	Tierney, J. (2009). *Criminology.* London: Longman.
Pears, R. and Shields, G. (2016) *Cite them right: The essential referencing guide.* 10th edn. Basingstoke: Palgrave Macmillan.	Tierney, J. (2009) *Criminology.* London: Longman.

Source: Biggam, J. (2018) *Succeeding with Your Master's Dissertation.* 4th edn. London: Open University Press.

Nonetheless, the advice in Pears and Shields' book *Cite Them Right* is understandably proving to be very popular in universities, evidenced by the fact that many departments have adopted it as a referencing guide for their students. The Harvard formatting advice given in this book adheres to that found in *Cite Them Right*. Where there are differences, an explanation is given.

Here are examples of how to format common sources found in a reference list. A summary template for formatting the different entries in a reference list, from art work to websites, is included in Appendix B (with examples).

Book

Author's surname, initials (year) *Title of book*. Edition if not first. Place of publication: Publisher.

Boland, A., Cherry, M. G. and Dickson, R. (2013) *Doing a systematic review*. London: SAGE.

Dreyfus, H. L. (2001) *On the internet*. London: Routledge.

Hoaglin, D. C. *et al.* (1982) *Data for decisions: Information strategies for policymakers*. Cambridge, MA: Abt Books.

Neville, C. (2016) *The complete guide to referencing and avoiding plagiarism*. 3rd edn. London: Open University Press.

Pears, R. and Shields, G. (2016) *Cite them right: The essential referencing guide*. 10th edn. Basingstoke: Palgrave Macmillan.

The Concise Oxford Dictionary (1988) 9th edn. London: BCA.

Note that the third example includes *et al. Cite Them Right* advises that where there are four or more authors, then list the first author – in this case Hoaglin, D. C. – and use the Latin term *et al.* (meaning 'and others') to cover the other authors. This is perfectly acceptable. However, if you are one of the 'and others', then you would not be best pleased: contributing authors understandably like to see their work credited. There is nothing wrong with replacing this with an expanded reference entry to include all contributing authors:

Hoaglin, D. C., Light, R. J., McPeak, B., Mosteller, F. and Stotos, M. A. (1982) *Data for decisions: Information strategies for policymakers*. Cambridge, MA: Abt Books.

In the body of your essay, you would be expected to cite this as Hoaglin *et al.* (1982) but it makes sense to give credit to all authors when you create your reference list.

Note that the sixth example shows you how to write a reference entry where there is no author. In which case the title of the book, *italicised*, appears in place of an author.

E-book

Author's surname, initials (year) *Title of book*. Available at: URL (Accessed: date).

Taylor, M. and Mayled, J. (2009) *OCR Philosophy of Religion*. Available at: https://smilewww.amazon.co.uk/OCR-Philosophy-Religion-AS-A2/dp/0415468248 (Accessed: 18 March 2017).

Conference paper[2]

If viewed offline:

Author's surname, initials (year) 'Title of paper', *Title of conference*, location, dates of conference. Place of publication: publisher, page(s).

Bloom, J. (2017) 'Picasso turns blue', *Straight from the artist's mouth*, Art Institute, Falkirk, 2–3 March 2015. London: Artbooks, pp. 36–40.

If viewed online:

Author's surname, initials (year) 'Title of paper', *Title of conference*, location, dates of conference, page(s) if available. Available at: URL (Accessed: date).

Conole, G., Oliver, M., Isroff, K. and Ravenscroft, A. (2004) 'Addressing methodological issues in e-learning research', *Proceedings of the Networked Learning Conference*, Lancaster University, UK, 5–7 April 2013.[3] Available at: www.sef.ac.uk/nlc/Proceedings/Symposa4.htm (Accessed: 2 October 2004).

Or (using *et al.*):

Conole, G. *et al.* (2004) 'Addressing methodological issues in e-learning research', *Proceedings of the Networked Learning Conference*, Lancaster University, UK, 5–7 April. Available at: www.sef.ac.uk/nlc/Proceedings/Symposa4.htm (Accessed: 2 October 2004).

Government publication (national-level)

If viewed offline:

Author's surname, initials (year) *Title of publication*, Place of publication: Publisher.

Goulding, A. and Cavanagh, B. (2013) *Charges reported under the Offensive Behaviour at Football and Threatening Communications (Scotland) Act in 2012–2013*, Edinburgh: Scottish Government Social Research.

If viewed online:

Author's surname, initials (year) *Title of publication*, Place of publication: Publisher. Available at: URL (Accessed: date).

Sosenko, F., Livingstone, N. and Fitzpatrick, S. (2013) *Overview of food aid provision in Scotland*, Edinburgh: Scottish Government Social Research. Available at: http://www.gov.scot/Resource/0044/00440458.pdf (Accessed: 23 July 2016).

When governments, or departments, outsource research (normally to universities), then the author name(s) will be credited in the government publication and so should be included in your reference.

Government publication (department-level)

If viewed offline:

Department/service/govt name (year) *Title of publication*, Place of publication: Publisher.

Justice Analytical Services (2013) *An examination of the evidence of sectarianism in Scotland*, Edinburgh: Scottish Government Social Research.

If viewed online:

Department/service/govt name (year) *Title of publication*, Place of publication: Publisher. Available at: URL (accessed: date).

Animal Health and Welfare Division (2013) *Promoting responsible dog ownership in Scotland: Microchipping and other measures*, Edinburgh: APS Group Scotland. Available at: http://www.gov.scot/Resource/0044/00441549.pdf (Accessed: 14 March 2014).

Many government publications are written internally by government departments and therefore author names are often unavailable, in which case you should give the name of the source department (Health Department) or service (e.g. Justice Analytical Services), or failing that, the government (e.g. Government of Canada) in place of author name(s).

Journal article

If viewed offline:

Author's surname, initials (year) 'Title of article', *Name of Journal*, volume number (issue number), page(s).

Burns, E. (1994) 'Information assets, technology and organisation', *Management Science*, 40(12), pp. 645–662.

Tearle, P., Dillon, P. and Davies, N. (1999) 'Use of information technology by English university teachers. Developments and trends at the time of the National Inquiry into Higher Education', *Journal of Further and Higher Education*, 23(1), pp. 5–15.[4]

If viewed online:

Author's surname, initials (year) 'Title of article', *Name of Journal*, volume number (issue number), page(s) if available. Available at: URL (accessed: date).

Gwatipeda, J. and Barbier, E. B. (2013) 'Environmental regulation of a global pollution externality in a bilateral trade environment: The case of global warming, China and the US', *Economics*, 2013 (60), pp. 1–43. Available at: http://www.economics-ejournal.org/economics/discussionpapers/2013-60 (Accessed: 18 August 2014).

Newspaper article

If viewed offline:

Author's surname, initials (year) 'Title of article', *Name of Newspaper*, day and month of publication, page(s).

If viewed offline and the author is known:

Riddell, P. and Webster, P. (2006) 'Support for Labour at lowest level since 1992', *The Times*, 9 May, p. 2.

If viewed offline and the author is not known:

The Indian Agra News (2007) 'Carbon footprints and economic globalisation', 18 April, p. 4.

If viewed online:

Author's surname, initials (year) 'Title of article', *Name of Newspaper*, day and month of publication. Available at: URL (accessed: date).

If viewed online and the author is known:

McArdle, H. (2013) 'Officials say new Forth bridge on schedule', *The Herald*, 30 December. Available at: http://www.heraldscotland.com/news/13138238. Officials_say_new_Forth_bridge_on_schedule/ (Accessed: 30 December 2013).

If viewed online and the author is not known:

The Herald (2013) 'Officials say new Forth bridge on schedule', 30 December. Available at: http://www.heraldscotland.com/news/13138238.Officials_say_new_Forth_bridge_on_schedule/(Accessed: 30 December 2013).

Theses and dissertations

If viewed offline:

Author's name, initials (year) *Title of thesis/dissertation*. Level of award. Institution.

Aitken, R. (2008) *Exploring the role of laughter in the workplace.* PhD thesis. Inverclyde University.

Denison, F. (2013) *Poetry and sedition.* Undergraduate dissertation. Inverclyde University.

If viewed online:

Author's name, initials (year) *Title of thesis/dissertation.* Level of award. Institution. Available at: URL (accessed: date).

Website

Author's name, initials (year) *Title of web page.* Available at: URL (Accessed: date).

Brender, A. (2004) *Speakers promote distance education to audiences in Asia.* Available at: www.chronicle.com (Accessed: 12 November 2015).

You might find that you have little information to write down, or that the content you once read on a website is no longer there. Do not worry: write down as much as you can at the time the link was available. If there is no author for the web article/source, then record the name of the website or organisation instead. For example:

The eLearning Centre (2005) *eLearning is taking giant steps,* etc.

You can record a source that is referred to in another source, for example, where you read in a book about a journal article and you want to cite the journal article. To record the example where Barlow, on page 634 of her book written in 2007, cites a journal article written by MacFarlane in 2004, and where you have also referred to MacFarlane in the body of your text, then you can note this information in your References section by first of all citing MacFarlane's journal article – because that is the source that most interests you – to which you add the phrase 'cited in', followed by Barlow's book in the normal way, as follows:

MacFarlane, K. (2004) 'Alternative approach to cognitive learning', *Organisational Learning*, 10(2), pp. 23–45, cited in Barlow, A. (2007) *Learning Again.* Buckingham: Open University Press, p. 634.

Suppose that you have read a book entitled *Classic and Cavalier: Essays on Jonson and the Sons of Ben.* This book consists of chapters written by different authors and you want to record the reference details for the chapter that was written by Martin Elsky, which appears from page 31 to page 44 in the book. You reference the chapter first, then indicate the general book details, as follows (this time just use *in* rather than *cited in* because the chapter appears *in* a book):

Elsky, M. (1982) 'Words, things, and names: Jonson's poetry and philosophical grammar', in Summers, C. J. and Pebworth, T. L. (eds) *Classic and cavalier: Essays on Jonson and the sons of Ben*. Pittsburgh, PA: University of Pittsburgh Press, pp. 31–44.

Citing and referencing sources are both a laborious, mechanical process but a necessary part of being viewed as an academic. The upside is that there are easy marks up for grabs; you need to take every opportunity to pick up easy marks. If your references are recent, relevant, and reliable, and plentiful in number, and you format them according to expected academic standards, then you are giving the clear impression that you are a top student. Top students get top marks. If, on the other hand, your references are sloppy, too few, and consist mainly of unscholarly web sources lacking in academic credibility, then your essay may come across as a poorly supported, if brilliantly written, opinion piece.

Remember, your audience is one academic (your marker), not your friends in a pub. Careful attention to citing sources and creating a robust reference list, using templates that meet your institution's expectations, will not only cut the mustard, it will do so with such panache that it will signal to your marker, in glowing neon lights: ACADEMIC AT WORK.

Summary of key points

- Plagiarism is where you take credit for someone else's work, in whole or in part, and claim it as your own. The antidote to plagiarism is referencing.
- You reference a source in two places in your essay: in-text (i.e. in the body of your essay) and in a reference list (i.e. at the end of your essay).
- For every source that you cite in-text, you need a corresponding entry – showing full publication details – in a reference list at the end of your essay.
- You can create a bibliography instead of a reference list, but there is no point in doing both. A bibliography will also contain sources that you have read but not cited in-text.
- There are different styles of referencing, each one designed to accommodate different disciplines. This book focuses on a multi-disciplinary style called Harvard referencing, also known as the author–date system.
- Even within different styles of referencing, including Harvard, there are variations on how to format a reference. This book follows the approach adopted in Pears and Shields' book, *Cite Them Right*.
- Your references ought to be (1) reasonably recent; (2) relevant; (3) reliable; (4) of sufficient quantity; and (5) formatted in line with academic standards.
- Referencing is a core skill expected of every academic. Ignoring this skill will undermine the credibility of your work. Developing it will enhance the status of your essay.

4 The hierarchy of essay questions

This chapter explains the relevance of Benjamin Bloom's theory of learning to your essay and, supported by Appendix C, highlights the *action words* used in essay questions to get you to do something. In short, there is a hierarchy to learning, from basic learning to advanced learning, and that hierarchy is expressed in the action words that appear in university essays.

Bloom's theory

It was that madcap genius Captain Beefheart who put forward the theory that there are only 40 people in this world and five of them are hamburgers. He was probably wrong. One theory that has stood the test of time, however, one that university markers use again and again, even if unwittingly, is a theory of learning put forward by Benjamin Bloom in his 1956 work, *Taxonomy of Educational Directives: The Classification of Educational Goals. Book 1: Cognitive Domain*. Bloom categorised the different layers of cognitive learning (the development of mental skills to acquire knowledge, i.e. your intellectual development). His categories have come to be known as *Bloom's taxonomy of learning domains* and are illustrated in the learning pyramid in Figure 4.1.

Bloom labelled the simplest level of learning as *knowledge*, and the highest as *evaluation*. The former referred to the acquisition of basic facts and figures, involving basic memory skills; the latter referred to an advanced level of learning, characterised by the ability to critically assess the views of others, using evidence to support your position. In between these two levels of learning there is an upward learning curve to get from acquiring basic *knowledge* to the stage where one can critically *evaluate* received wisdom. This journey involves picking up skills in comprehension (i.e. the ability to summarise material in your own words), application (i.e. the ability to relate theory to practice using examples),

Figure 4.1 Bloom's taxonomy of (cognitive) learning

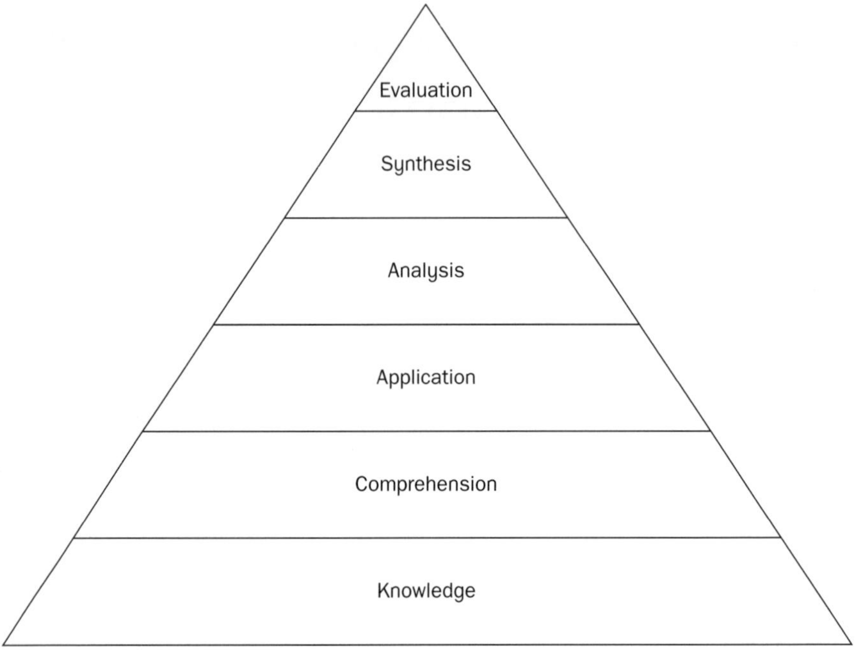

Source: Based on Bloom, B. (1956) *Taxonomy of Educational Directives: The Classification of Educational Goals. Book 1: Cognitive Domain.* New York: Longman.

analysis (i.e. the ability to deconstruct arguments and identify key issues), and synthesis (i.e. the ability to bring together strands of thought, producing a coherent position).

What has Bloom's taxonomy of learning domains got to do with university essays? Let's relate this hierarchy of learning to your essay.[1] An essay is the main instrument used in universities to test a student's understanding of an academic discipline. It is not the only testing tool available to universities. Others include, but are not limited to, multiple-choice questions, lab work, reports, learning logs, oral presentations, role play, and simulations. Essay questions are written to test particular *levels of learning*. These levels of learning, by and large, map quite neatly onto Bloom's theory of learning. The higher up the hierarchy of learning you go, the deeper your understanding of a subject area. That being so, a hierarchy of essay questions is created to test whether a student has achieved an expected level of intellectual development. Table 4.1 highlights the type of evidence that is normally sought in a university essay to reflect the different stages of learning expected of students.

At the higher end of the hierarchy of essay questions, your marker will go through your essay looking to find evidence of higher-level cognitive skills (such as *analysis*, *synthesis*, and *evaluation*). In such a scenario, if you stick to low-level cognitive skills (such as *knowledge* and basic *comprehension*), when

Table 4.1   Sample evidence of cognitive skills in your essay (and dissertation, for that matter)

Cognitive skill	Evidence (in your essay)
1 Knowledge	Repeating what you have heard in a lecture, writing down simple facts and figures, or quoting other authors. (So, basic memory skills, but no evidence that you understood what you wrote about.)
2 Comprehension	Paraphrasing what you have heard (in a lecture) or read summarising material in your own words, thereby illustrating simple comprehension skills.
3 Application	Taking someone's idea, view, or theory and giving a practical example to show that you can apply this. In other words, showing that you can relate theory to the real world.
4 Analysis	Breaking down arguments into constituent parts, dissecting an author's logic, identifying key issues in reports, surveys, articles, etc.
5 Synthesis	Bringing together strands of your argument and discussion, voiced at different stages in your essay, to create a coherent message to the reader.
6 Evaluation	Critically evaluating the work of other authors – combining a variety of the cognitive skills – and giving opinions with justifications. (So, presenting evidence of your ability to understand what you are reading.)

Source: Biggam, J. (2018) *Succeeding with Your Master's Dissertation*. 4th edn. London: Open University Press.

the essay question demands evidence of higher-level skills, then you will get low marks; if you exhibit higher-level cognitive skills, then you will secure higher marks. Table 4.1 provides examples of evidence for each of these cognitive skills, ranging from 1–6 in increasing order of importance.

How do you know which cognitive skill to focus on? Not all essay questions ask you to evaluate something. Sometimes an essay question is straightforward and only requires that you describe something and provide examples of that something in practice. On other occasions, an essay question might be split in two, with one part (the easy part) requiring a description of something or a summary of events, and the second part (the more demanding part) inviting you to identify key issues. Then again, other essays are clearly aimed at the top end of the cognitive pyramid, with the expectation that you will critically evaluate something. How do you know which cognitive skill, or skills, you are being tested on? Essay questions are not written any old way. The language used is deliberate. An essay question asks you to perform a particular task (or tasks).

The level of that task is indicated by the use of a verb, such as *identify, describe, analyse, evaluate*, etc. Verbs typically describe an action (e.g. she *walked* home), a condition (e.g. he *kept* quiet), or an experience (e.g. she *felt* sad). In the context of essay questions, the verbs that are asking you to do something (i.e. perform an action) are called 'action words'. The next section lists the different types of action words used in essay questions, directs you to definitions for them (so that you know what is expected of you), and illustrates their use through sample essay questions.

Action words

Just as there is a hierarchy of learning skills, so too there is a hierarchy of essay questions to reflect those skills. It is the *action words* in essay questions that dictate the level of learning that is being tested and, therefore, the level of answer that is expected. Remember, an action word is a verb that identifies the type of task that you are being asked to perform. Understanding action words is fundamental to producing an answer that meets your tutor's expectations. Different action words mean different things and if you ignore, or fail to grasp, what a particular action word is asking you to do, then it is unlikely that you will succeed in fulfilling the requirements of the essay. Let's now enter the world of action words and explore what they mean and the implications for your essay. Table 4.2 captures most of the action words used in university essays.

To show what they look like in context, here is a list of sample essay questions, each with the action word(s) *italicised* for emphasis:

1 *Account for* the rise of Fascism in 1930s Italy.
2 *Explain* the role of the Health and Safety Executive (HSE).
3 *With reference to* Marina Abramovic, *assess* the notion that performance art has an important contribution to make to contemporary art.
4 In the context of 20th-Century art, *interpret* what Robert Hughes meant by the phrase 'the shock of the new'.
5 *Examine* the case for the return of corporal punishment in the UK.
6 *Outline* the theory of constraints and *apply* it to an aspect of health care. *Discuss* your findings.
7 *What* causes mass hysteria?
8 *Differentiate* between the Scottish and English legal systems.
9 *Analyse* the contribution trade unions make to society.
10 *Comment* on the view that Einstein was a poor mathematician, *justifying* your answer with examples.
11 *Discuss* the importance of systematic reviews in medical research.
12 *Classify* the psychiatric taxonomy of mental disorders produced by the World Health Organization.
13 *Annotate* a diagram to *show* the stages of the Soft Systems Methodology.

Table 4.2 Action words used in university essays

Account for	Analyse	Annotate	Apply	Argue against	Argue for
Assess	Calculate	Choose	Clarify	Classify	Comment
Compare	Contrast	Consider	Critically . . .	Criticise	Critique
Deduce	Defend	Define	Demonstrate	Describe	Determine
Develop	Diagrammatically	Differentiate	Discuss	Distinguish	Elaborate
Enumerate	Evaluate	Examine	Expand	Explain	Explore
Extrapolate	How	How far	Identify	Illustrate	Infer
Interpolate	Interpret	Justify	List	Outline	Propose
Prove	Relate	Review	Select	Show (how)	State
Summarise	To what extent	Trace	Use	Use a diagram	Verify
What	When	Where	Which	Why	With reference to

14 *Evaluate* the usefulness of social media as a marketing tool.

15 *Critique* Freud's model of personality.

16 *Assess* the wisdom of the 2003 invasion of Iraq.

17 *Using* recent case law from Employment Tribunals and EU Directives, *determine* the criteria to qualify for employee status.

18 *Consider* the benefits, or otherwise, of group-work in student assignments.

19 *Trace* the causes of the First World War.

20 *Critically analyse* Hitchcock's use of story-shaping in *Rear Window*.

As you can see, sometimes there is more than one action word in an essay question (see examples 3, 6, 10, 13, and 17). In such circumstances, the first action word is typically a simple task (e.g. *with reference to, outline, comment on, annotate, using,* etc.), while the second action word tends to involve an in-depth activity (e.g. *discuss, assess, justifying, show,* and *determine,* etc.). If there are more than two action words in an essay question, as in example 6, then you need to consider what each action word means in order to determine their weighting relative to one another:

> *Outline* the theory of constraints and *apply* it to an aspect of health care. *Discuss* your findings.

This now brings us on to the matter of the meaning of individual action words. The following list shows definitions for some of the action words that appear in Table 4.2. All of the definitions for each of the action words listed in Table 4.2 are available in tabular form in Appendix C for easy reference.

Analyse. Examine in detail by breaking a subject down into its constituent parts, identifying and explaining the main characteristics of these parts and the nature of the relationship between the parts, including implications.

Assess. Estimate the worth/value of something by weighing up the advantages and disadvantages or strengths and weaknesses or arguments for and against.

Clarify. Make clear, shed light on.

Classify. Label or group things based on distinguishing characteristics.

Deduce. Arrive at a logical conclusion from a reasoned argument.

Demonstrate. Convince using clear explanations and examples.

Describe. Capture the main features of something or relate an event in detail.

Explain. Bring clarity to a topic by defining and interpreting what something means and/or provide detailed reasons for its occurrence (how and why) and/or implications.

Explore. Investigate a topic in detail, casting an inquisitive and probing eye, discussing options and implications. *Explore* questions are normally associated with scenarios, real or imagined.

Identify. Pinpoint the main causes/features of, or options/solutions to, something.

Illustrate. Make clear through the use of examples and/or diagrams.
Outline. Give a summary/sketch of main points/general features only.
Prove. Demonstrate the truth of a claim through rigorous argument using supporting evidence.
Review. Go over something with a critical eye, explaining its merits or otherwise, justifying points made.

Action words can be broken down (or *analysed*) into three rough categories, reflecting a hierarchy of tasks: Basic, Intermediate, and Advanced. Examples of *basic* action words (requiring basic tasks) are: comment, define, list and outline. Examples of *intermediate* action words (requiring an answer that is between basic and advanced) include: clarify, consider, describe, illustrate, and interpret. Examples of *advanced* action words (requiring an in-depth answer) include: analyse, assess, discuss, evaluate, and review.

Note that when a basic action word appears in an essay question, it is usually followed by an intermediate or advanced action word:

> *Choose* a contemporary Scottish poet and *explain* the significance of their work.

> *Outline* the stages of the Waterfall model and *assess* its usefulness as a systems development methodology.

Also note that the classification of an action word is not set in stone and the boundaries between one grouping and another can be fluid, depending on the context. Nonetheless, the key message to take away is that if you are asked to *evaluate* something and you merely *outline* it, then you have not done what has been asked of you and your mark will therefore be lower. Similarly, if you have been asked to *outline* something and you *evaluate* it, then you have misunderstood the task in hand and your mark will suffer. More typically, students tend to *describe* when they have been asked to *discuss* or *evaluate*; or, where two action words appear in an essay question, one of which suggests a basic task (e.g. *outline*) and the other an advanced task (e.g. *evaluate*), students erroneously give more weight to the easier task.

 A common student mistake

A common mistake by students is to ignore the meaning attached to an action word and, as a matter of course, lunge headlong into a descriptive exercise.

Very often an action word will be preceded by the adverb *briefly* or, at the other end of the action-word scale, the adverb *critically*. Remember, from Chapter 3, an adverb is a word that modifies a verb: *briefly* explain, *critically* evaluate, etc. (although traditional grammarians would argue that the adverb should appear after the verb). The former is used to emphasise that a short answer is expected and the latter that an in-depth one is expected. For example, although *discuss* suggests an in-depth answer, *briefly discuss* is telling you to calm your beans. Sometimes the adverb *briefly* is in practice redundant and is there purely for emphasis (e.g. *briefly outline* or *briefly comment*). The adverb *critically* is nearly always used for emphasis, and frequently appears in front of *assess*, *evaluate*, and *review*: *critically assess*, *critically evaluate*, *critically review*. In reality, there is no difference between *assess* and *critically assess*; *evaluate* and *critically evaluate*; *review* and *critically review*. For example, there is no difference between the following two essay questions, other than as a helpful reminder:

1   *Review* Guy Hollands' stage production of Beckett's *Waiting for Godot*.
2   *Critically review* Guy Hollands' stage production of Beckett's *Waiting for Godot*.

The adverb *critically* does not mean to criticise (i.e. to exclusively find fault with). It has a wider meaning in academia: to give an in-depth, informed, and balanced discussion on the merits or otherwise of something. When you review something, you go over it with an analytical eye, explaining its merits or otherwise, justifying points made. In other words, critically review = review. Similarly, *critically assess* = *assess* and *critically evaluate* = *evaluate*. That said, *critically* is a helpful reminder to the student.

The advanced action words used – *analyse*, *assess*, *discuss*, *evaluate*, *review*, etc. – are often misunderstood by students. For many students, their default position is to ignore what the advanced action word is asking them to do and instead to drop down to an intermediate level answer that they are comfortable with, namely, *describing* things, with only a token sentence or two tagged on towards the end of their essay hinting at a higher-level task. Students who adopt this position can, at best, only hope for a mid-range mark. Yet, with some advice on how to tackle advanced action words, this temptation towards mediocrity can be turned round.

The lesson in this chapter is to appreciate that as you go through university, the essay questions become more demanding and this is reflected in the action words used. As soon as you get your essay question, highlight the action word(s), look up the definition(s) to make sure that you know what is expected of you, and if there is more than one action word, then give more weight to the higher-level task. This process is outlined in Table 4.3.

One final point. It is interesting to note that essay questions often do not contain a question at all! For example, *Discuss the causes of the First World War* is not a question but an instruction to you, the student, to do something. Nonetheless, the instruction can be interpreted as effectively *asking you* 'What are the causes of the First World War?'. Hence the long-standing allusion to 'essay questions'. Of course, many essay questions are in the form of a blatant question (e.g. *What do you understand by the term postmodernism?*) or are a combination of question and instruction (e.g. *Why is art important? Provide*

Table 4.3 Highlighting action words

Stage	Process	Example
1	Receive essay question.	Outline the causes of child poverty and critically review the Scottish Government's proposals for tackling child poverty.
2	Highlight action word(s) (use highlighter pen, underline, or bold).	**Outline** the causes of child poverty and **critically review** the Scottish Government's proposals for tackling child poverty.
3	Define this/these task(s).	**Outline**: Give a summary/sketch of main points/general features. **Critically review**: Go over something with a critical eye explaining its merits or otherwise, justifying points made.
4	Relate definition(s) back to essay question.	**Outline**: Give a summary/sketch of main points/general features *of the causes of child poverty*. **Critically review**: Go over *the Scottish Government's proposals for tackling child poverty* with a critical eye explaining its merits or otherwise, justifying points made.
5	More than one action word? Emphasise the higher-level skill. If action words are basic action words (or all intermediate action words), then give equal weighting to each task in your answer (unless marks suggest otherwise).	Reminder to myself: the focus of essay should be on critically reviewing the Scottish Government's approach to tackling child poverty (rather than outlining the causes of child poverty).

examples to illustrate your views). Besides, 'essay questions' is a neutral academic term that is more palatable than the harsh-sounding 'essay instructions' – or, worse, 'essay commands'!

There are other stages involved in deconstructing an essay question – these are covered in detail in Chapter 5.

Summary of key points

- Benjamin Bloom (1956) highlighted different levels of learning, from acquiring basic knowledge to the highest intellectual development characterised by the ability to evaluate information.
- This hierarchy of learning is reflected in university marking schemes: basic knowledge gets basic marks; evidence of higher-level skills gets higher marks.
- To indicate which level of answer markers are expecting in student essays, action words are used.
- Action words are the verbs in an essay question that indicate what you have to do with the topic under discussion (examples include *account for*, *explain*, and *describe*).
- Different action words indicate different levels of answer. These can roughly be divided into three categories: basic action words (e.g. annotate, outline, and sketch), intermediate action words (e.g. describe, explain, and interpret), and advanced action words (e.g. assess, analyse, and review).
- Where two or more action words appear in an essay question, more weighting should be given to the higher-level action word (it is unlikely that more than one higher-level action word will appear in the same essay question, given the depth of answer that each demands). Where the action words are all basic action words, or all intermediate action words, then give equal weighting in your answer to each action word.
- When you get your 'essay question', make sure that you understand what the action words mean. If you follow the process outlined in Table 4.3, then that should get you off to a good start.

Part **2**

Planning and building a good university essay

5 Step 1: Deconstruct the essay question using GALA

Pre-stage
Deconstruct the essay question
The absent action word

This chapter takes you through the first step to answering an essay question: deconstructing your essay question.

Pre-stage

There are five main steps in writing a university essay:

Step 1: Deconstruct the essay question
Step 2: Create a roadmap
Step 3: Introduce your essay
Step 4: Write the Main Body
Step 5: Conclude your essay

This chapter takes you through Step 1. However, prior to Step 1, you should get hold of a marking scheme (where one exists). Although it is unlikely that you will find a marking scheme for individual essays, most universities produce a generic marking scheme to help academics convert their academic judgement into a numerical mark. A generic marking scheme is one that can be used within a department, if not across departments and faculties, or indeed the whole university, for multiple assessments.

Generic marking schemes can differ from university to university, but what is typical is a statement of the criteria required to achieve a mark associated with a particular grade. Assuming that you are aiming for an 'A-grade' mark, then it makes sense that you understand the criteria for achieving that grade. A copy of the marking scheme would help you to understand how to achieve

Table 5.1   Example generic marking scheme

Grade	Mark	Description	Criteria
A	70–100	EXCELLENT	Shows comprehensive understanding of subject matter, evidenced by independent critical thought, linking theory to practice using a wide variety of sources. Well-structured, coherent and insightful argument supported by a full reference list consistent with high academic standards.
B	60–69	VERY GOOD	
C	50–59	GOOD	
D	40–49	PASS	
E	30–39	NARROW FAIL	
F	0–29	FAIL	

that aim. For example, suppose that the generic marking scheme indicates the criteria for an A grade seen in Table 5.1.

The generic marking scheme tends to be based on the degree classifications for first-class degree (70+), upper-second (60–69), lower-second (50–59), third-class (40–49), etc. So, even if your department does not make use of a generic marking scheme, have a look at the degree classifications, and associated criteria, and you will get a good idea of the standard that you need to reach to be viewed as an academic high flyer.

Although you will be deconstructing your essay question in order to work out precisely what you are being asked to do, there is merit in keeping in mind your department's view of what it takes, in general, to achieve a mark of 70+. Extract that criteria and create a basic spider diagram (a central circle with spidery lines coming out) to separate and highlight the key components that collectively evidence an A-grade student.

Let's suppose that the generic criteria for 70+ is as stated in Table 5.1. In the first instance, extract the relevant text from the generic marking scheme:

> Shows comprehensive understanding of subject matter, evidenced by independent critical thought, linking theory to practice using a wide variety of sources. Well-structured, coherent and insightful argument supported by a full reference list consistent with high academic standards.

Then draw a basic spider diagram to show what it takes to get 70+ (Figure 5.1).

Figure 5.1 Quick spider diagram highlighting A-grade criteria

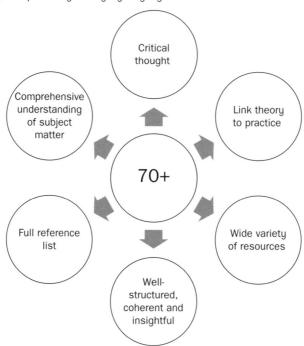

All of that only takes about 15 minutes at most and it has the benefit of making you aware of the general criteria that need to be met to achieve an A grade. Keep this handy when you write your essay. In that way, you can remind yourself of the evidence required to justify the high mark that you seek. Now let's look at the mechanics of writing a university essay, starting with how to deconstruct an essay question.

Deconstruct the essay question

When you deconstruct something, you break it down into its constituent parts, which, in turn, allows you to understand how that thing was put together in the first place. In this way, deconstruction provides insight. In the context of a university essay question, deconstruction reveals what the person who set the question wants you to do. If you know what precisely is being asked of you, then you are starting from an excellent position (and you are increasing your chances of being awarded an 'excellent' grade!). Unfortunately, too many students skip the deconstruction part and go straight to trying to write their essay, without a clear understanding of what they need to do and in what order.

A common student mistake

A common mistake by students is to ignore the nuances of an essay question and write in general terms about a subject area, only belatedly touching upon main issues that ought to have been addressed earlier and in detail.

To help us deconstruct an essay question, we can make use of a model called GALA. Imagine that you have been given the following essay assignment.

Example 1

Assess the part that de-regulation played in the 2008 banking crisis.

Table 5.2 shows a simple deconstruction model for an essay question. The model has the name GALA, which is an abbreviated reminder of the four questions that will help you to deconstruct an essay question.

Applying GALA to our sample essay question, *Assess the part that de-regulation played in the 2008 banking crisis:*

G: What is the **G**eneral topic area? The general topic in our sample question is the **banking crisis**: '*Assess the part that de-regulation played in the 2008 **banking crisis**.*'

A: What **A**spect of the main topic (in this case, the banking crisis) is to be addressed? You have been asked to write about **de-regulation**, specifically the part it played in the banking crisis: '*Assess the **part that de-regulation played** in the 2008 banking crisis.*'

L: What words **L**imit your essay to particular time periods or geographical areas (etc.)? In this case, the limiting text is '*2008*': '*Assess the part that de-regulation played in the **2008** banking crisis.*'

Table 5.2 Deconstructing an essay question using the GALA template

Essay Question:	
	Question Deconstruction
General topic area:	
Aspect of general topic to be addressed:	
Limiting word(s):	
Action word(s):	

A: Lastly, what **A**ction words are used? An action word is a word that indicates the type of writing activity that you are required to perform. Examples of action words are: *assess, describe, evaluate, outline, review*, and *summarise*. The action word in the sample essay question is 'assess': '**Assess** *the part that de-regulation played in the 2008 banking crisis.*'

We are now in a position to fill in the blanks for our GALA deconstruction model (Table 5.3).

Next, you need to understand the meaning of your action word used, in this case *assess* (we have been here before: you will find definitions of action words in Appendix C).

Assess: Estimate the worth/value of something by weighing up the advantages and disadvantages or strengths and weaknesses or arguments for and against.

Next, translate the action word into the context of the essay question. Don't be scared to reinterpret the essay question in light of the definition of the action word. Students do it in their head anyway when they get an essay question. All you are doing is putting your thoughts down in writing, but from an informed basis. In this case, *assess* has the following meaning:

Assess: Estimate the extent to which de-regulation played a part in the banking crisis by weighing up the arguments for and against that view.

You can now see the benefit of deconstructing your essay question. Not only are you being forced to focus on the specific aspect of a general topic, taking into account limiting factors, but you now know how to interpret the actual task.

Let's get more practice using GALA using four more examples.

Table 5.3 Applying GALA (Example 1)

Essay Question: *Assess the part that de-regulation played in the 2008 banking crisis.*

	Question Deconstruction
General topic area:	*banking crisis*
Aspect of general topic to be addressed:	*de-regulation*
Limiting word(s):	*2008*
Action word(s):	*Assess*

Example 2

> *Account for the rise of Fascism in 1930s Italy.*

Apply the GALA template (Table 5.4). For convenience the definition of the action word has been placed in the GALA template alongside the action word.
Rewriting the essay question using the definition of 'account for' gives us:

> *Provide an explanation for the rise of Fascism in 1930s Italy.*

Table 5.4 Applying GALA (Example 2)

Essay Question: *Account for the rise of Fascism in 1930s Italy.*

	Question Deconstruction
General topic area:	*Fascism*
Aspect of general topic to be addressed:	*rise of Fascism*
Limiting word(s):	*1930s Italy*
Action word(s):	*Account for*: to provide an explanation or reason for something.

Example 3

> *Outline the theory of constraints and apply it to an aspect of health care. Discuss your findings.*

Apply the GALA template (Table 5.5).
This example raises a number of points:

1 There is no limiting word. That's not a problem. Although many essay questions restrict the scope of a question in terms of, for example, geographical location or time frame, that is not the case here.
2 More than one action word is used. When that happens, weight your answer to the higher-level tasks. In order of simplest first, the three action words (i.e. tasks) are *outline, apply*, and *discuss*. That is because *outline* is a basic task, *apply* is an intermediate task, and *discuss* is an advanced task. This means that you spend more time on the discussion part than the application part, and more time on the application part than the outline part.

Reinterpreting the essay question in light of the definitions of the three action words:

> Original question: Outline the theory of constraints and apply it to an aspect of health care. Discuss your findings.

Table 5.5 Applying GALA (Example 3)

Essay Question: *Outline the theory of constraints and apply it to an aspect of health care. Discuss your findings.*

	Question Deconstruction
General topic area:	*theory of constraints*
Aspect of general topic to be addressed:	*applied in health care*
Limiting word(s):	–
Action word(s):	*Outline*: give a summary/sketch of main points/ general features only.
	Apply: show through the use of relevant examples.
	Discuss: to debate an issue in the round, i.e. from different perspectives, including pros and cons, for and against, advantages and disadvantages, and so coming to a balanced conclusion.

Interpretation: Summarise the general features of the theory of constraints and show an example of it in one aspect of health care. Use your findings to debate the arguments for and against the theory of constraints.

Example 4

With reference to three paintings of your choice, describe the main characteristics of Impressionism.

Apply the GALA template (Table 5.6).
Reinterpretation of essay question in light of definition of action word:

With reference to three paintings of your choice, capture, in detail, the main characteristics of Impressionism.[1]

Example 5

Evaluate the usefulness of social media as a marketing tool.

Apply the GALA template (Table 5.7).
Reinterpretation of essay question in light of definition of action word:

Judge the worth of social media as a marketing tool by appraising its benefits and limitations, using reliable sources as evidence.[2]

Table 5.6   Applying GALA (Example 4)

Essay Question: *With reference to three paintings of your choice, describe the main characteristics of Impressionism.*	
	Question Deconstruction
General topic area:	*Impressionism*
Aspect of general topic to be addressed:	*main characteristics*
Limiting word(s):	*With reference to three paintings*
Action word(s):	*Describe*: capture the main features of something or relate an event in detail.

Table 5.7   Applying GALA (Example 5)

Essay Question: *Evaluate the usefulness of social media as a marketing tool.*	
	Question Deconstruction
General topic area:	*social media*
Aspect of general topic to be addressed:	*usefulness*
Limiting word(s):	*marketing tool*
Action word(s):	*Evaluate*: Judge the worth – value – of something by appraising its benefits and limitations, using reliable sources as evidence.

The absent action word

There will be occasions where the action word in an essay question appears to be missing. Most essay questions are statements and not questions (i.e. they do not end in a question mark). The absence of an obvious action word is a rare occasion but normally occurs where the essay question is not a statement but is, in fact, a question. Most essay questions of this type start with 'What...' or 'How...' or 'Why...'. *What, how,* and *why* are action words and ought to be interpreted as such, each of which is defined in Appendix C. Less obvious is the question that does not start with *what* or *how* or *why*, as in:

Do you agree that elitism is a destructive force in society?

In such circumstances, you are being asked to come to a conclusion in the affirmative or the negative after weighing up the arguments for and against something. Interpret such questions as asking you to *assess* the validity of a statement. The definition of *assess* is: estimate the worth/value of something by weighing up the advantages and disadvantages or strengths and weaknesses or arguments for and against.

Appendix D contains the template for GALA and is supported by further examples. As you can see, this chapter recommends that you deconstruct your essay question in two phases:

1 Apply GALA.
2 Rewrite the essay question using the definition of any action word(s).

By doing so, you will be in a better position to understand the tasks that you have been asked to do. It is from that deconstruction that you will derive the structure of your essay. Deconstructing the essay question is therefore the first step to writing your essay. It is an important step and one that should not be overlooked. The next step takes the results of Step 1 and shows you how to create a roadmap (structure) for your essay.

Summary of key points

- Before you begin your essay, get hold of the departmental generic marking scheme (where one exists). It will help you appreciate what you need to do in your essays to be awarded an A-grade.
- The first stage in writing a university essay is to deconstruct the essay question. GALA is a template that will break down the essay question into **G**eneral topic, **A**spect of general topic, **L**imiting conditions, and **A**ction word(s) to be applied, allowing you to get a clearer understanding of the task ahead.
- Once you have completed the deconstruction table, you should then rewrite the essay question, making use of action word definitions.

6 Step 2: Create a roadmap

Pre-stage
Create a roadmap

This chapter takes you through Step 2 of writing a university essay: how to create a roadmap for your essay, starting with the importance of a roadmap and practical advice on how to prepare for this activity.

Pre-stage

Writing a university essay can be broken down into five steps. We have already covered Step 1 on how to deconstruct an essay question. This chapter focuses on Step 2: using information obtained from Step 1 to create a roadmap:

Step 1:   Deconstruct the essay question ✓
Step 2:   Create a roadmap
Step 3:   Introduce your essay
Step 4:   Write the Main Body
Step 5:   Conclude your essay

An essay is a journey. Like any journey, you need to know how to prepare for what lies ahead: where to start, where you want to end up, the route that best meets your needs, and how to deal with obstacles. The alternative is to start your journey without any planning, meander about here and there, asking people you meet along the way if you are on the right track, and hope that the place you are looking for will suddenly appear over the horizon. Unfortunately, when it comes to writing essays, the alternative scenario is the reality for many students.

The way to know how to get to where you want to go is to use a roadmap. In the context of an essay, the roadmap is your essay structure. The advantages of working out a structure for your essay are too many to ignore:

- the shape of your essay becomes evident;
- the number, order, and weight of tasks are laid out before you;
- you can apportion time to individual tasks;
- it is easier to work out completion time;
- the labelled/headed tasks keep you on track;
- the tasks directly relate to the essay question;
- completing the tasks, completes the essay question.

In short, having a roadmap keeps you focused on the journey that you have been asked to complete and saves you time.

> **! A common student mistake**
>
> A common mistake by students is to pay scant attention to creating a road-map. The result is *student drift* (i.e. wandering away from what should be the focus of the essay).

Your essay structure is essentially your headings. These headings signpost the terrain you will be covering and the direction your essay will take. Once you complete your essay, you can remove the headings if you wish or leave them as a guide to others. Retaining headings shows your marker that you understand the requirements of the essay question and, where questions are divided into parts (a) and (b) or more, you are helpfully indicating where in your essay you have answered these parts.

How do you create your roadmap? That's easy. As you will soon see, there is a generic essay structure that is common to all academic essays (i.e. they must have a beginning, middle, end, and references) but to get from the general essay structure to one that is specific to your essay question requires:

1 the application of GALA;
2 a reinterpretation of the essay question making use of action word definitions.

As we explored in Chapter 5, GALA breaks down the essay question into **G**eneral topic, **A**spect of that topic to be covered, **L**imiting words, and **A**ction(s) to be carried out. Understanding what that action is lets you know what you are required to do with the topic(s). From these two activities your essay structure will become evident. Thus, before working out a roadmap for your essay, you ought to have in front of you the GALA template (Table 6.1) and action word definitions (Appendix C).

A practical approach would be to create a new document in your word processor, write your essay question at the top, place the GALA template below the

Table 6.1 Deconstructing an essay question using the GALA template

Essay Question:	
	Question Deconstruction
General topic area:	
Aspect of general topic to be addressed:	
Limiting word(s):	
Action word(s):	

Figure 6.1 Preparing to create your essay roadmap

Essay Question:	
	Question Deconstruction
General topic area:	
Aspect of general topic to be addressed:	
Limiting words(s):	
Action words(s):	

Rewriting essay question (using action word[s] definitions[s]):

Essay structure:

essay question, leave a space below that to rewrite the essay question (making use of action word definitions), and, below that, leave a space to enter your essay structure (Figure 6.1).

Create a roadmap

A roadmap tells you how to get to where you want to go. Here's how to create one for your essay.

There are two types of templates that we will make use of: the generic and the specific. The former is a general outline and works for any essay; the latter is dependent on the specifics of your essay question. View the general template as the aerial street map of a town you want to visit for a night or two, and the specific template as the route to take to get to your hotel. Let's deal with the general template first.

All essays have a beginning, middle, and end (Figure 6.2).

Another way of writing this is to think of the role played by each of these essay parts. The purpose of the beginning is to introduce your essay. That's why it's called an *introduction*. Step 3 of the roadmap (covered in Chapter 7) will tell you how to write an introduction but the main thing to remember for now is that the introduction is where you tell the reader what you are going to write about; not only that, you are also upfront and say what your position is (this is called your *thesis*). The end of your essay is more commonly referred to as your *conclusion* because it is where you reflect on what you wrote and reiterate your main thesis. You might also want to make a recommendation or leave your reader with some food for thought. The chunk in the middle of your essay is called the *main body*, or *body* if you prefer. That's where you make your main points or arguments, with each point leading smoothly into the next point, thereby convincing the reader of your position. You must support each of your points with evidence (usually a combination of sources and compelling argument). Your sources are listed at the end of your essay. An updated generic template now appears in Figure 6.3.

To get back to basics, you can view the Introduction, Main Body, and Conclusion as shown succinctly in Figure 6.4.

First, a word about word-length for each of these parts. It is generally accepted that the 10:80:10 percentage rule applies to university essays. That is, 10 per cent of the available words is spent on the Introduction, 80 per cent on

Figure 6.2 Generic essay template: Beginning, middle, and end

Figure 6.3 Generic essay template: Introduction, Main Body, Conclusion, and References

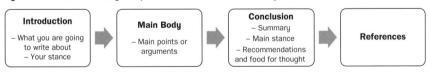

Figure 6.4 Generic essay template: Back to basics

the Main Body, and the remaining 10 per cent on the Conclusion. The reference list is not normally included in the word count. So, if you have a 2,000-word essay to write, then the portion of words is 200 towards the Introduction; 1,800 on the Main Body; and 200 on the Conclusion.

The 10:80:10 rule is not carved in stone, it is just a guideline. The reality is that most Introductions take less than 10 per cent of the words available and that the Conclusion is usually longer than the Introduction because it has the added job of summarising the main points. Your specific essay structure will depend on the essay question but it will still be based on the generic template, shown in Figure 6.3. Let's revisit essay questions where we have applied GALA to see how to get from the generic essay structure to one specific to your essay question.

Example 1

Assess the part that de-regulation played in the 2008 banking crisis.

Apply the GALA template (Table 6.2). For convenience, the definition of the action word has been placed in the GALA template alongside the action word itself.

Rewriting the essay question using the definition of the action word (in this case, *assess*), gives us:

Estimate the extent to which de-regulation played a part in the 2008 banking crisis by weighing up the arguments for and against that view.

From a combination of: (1) the generic structure; (2) the GALA Table 6.2; and (3) the reinterpretation of the essay question, we can now derive a solid road-map for our essay. From (1) the generic structure, we have:

- Introduction
- Main Points/Arguments
- Conclusion
- References

From (2) the GALA Table 6.2, we see that the general topic area is the banking crisis. Well, let's have some background information on the banking crisis (e.g. what it was and when it occurred) to set the scene:

- Introduction
- Background: The Banking Crisis
- Main Points/Arguments
- Conclusion
- References

From Table 6.2, we also see that the specific topic is de-regulation. It's always good to define terms. So, let's clarify what we mean by de-regulation:

Table 6.2 Applying GALA (Example 1)

Essay Question: *Assess the part that de-regulation played in the 2008 banking crisis.*

	Question Deconstruction
General topic area:	banking crisis
Aspect of general topic to be addressed:	de-regulation
Limiting word(s):	*2008*
Action word(s):	Assess: Estimate the worth/value of something by weighing up the advantages and disadvantages or strengths and weaknesses or arguments for and against.

- Introduction
- Background: The Banking Crisis
- Definition: De-regulation
- Main Points/Arguments
- Conclusion
- References

Next, we look at (3) the reinterpretation of the essay question based on what the action word *assess* means. Remember, after inserting the meaning of the action word, the reinterpretation of the essay question was:

> *Estimate the extent to which de-regulation played a part in the 2008 banking crisis by weighing up the arguments for and against that view.*

This means that the spine of our main body will concentrate on the arguments for blaming de-regulation for the banking crisis and the arguments against blaming de-regulation for the banking crisis, giving us a final essay structure:

- Introduction
- Background: The Banking Crisis
- Definition: De-regulation
- De-regulation to Blame for the Banking Crisis?
- The Banking Crisis: Other Factors?
- Conclusion
- References

You could, if you want, combine an outline of the banking crisis (i.e. what it was) followed by what you understand by the term *de-regulation* under the same heading: Background Information. Remember, whereas background information helps to set the scene and is nearly always of benefit to your reader, it is not always the case that you need to define terms.

Having headings in your essay, at least during the writing process, will keep you on the straight and narrow. A common complaint by tutors when marking essays is that many students spend too much time on describing background information and not enough time on the main discussion points. By inserting headings, you, in effect, move the basic information to the beginning of your essay.

It is worth repeating that whether or not you decide to keep the headings once you complete your essay is largely personal choice, but doing so lets the marker know that you have a carefully constructed structure and, importantly, that you understand what the essay question is asking you to do. Also, as stated earlier, there is another practical reason for retaining headings in your final essay: sometimes an essay question is clearly divided into parts (a) and (b), or more, and headings allow you to address specifically these parts in a focused way. Indeed, two or more action words in an essay question effectively indicate two or more parts to be addressed (e.g. *outline . . .* and *evaluate . . .*). Headings therefore act as a reminder to tackle specific tasks highlighted in the essay question.

Taking into account the usefulness of background information to set the scene, we now have an updated generic essay structure (Figure 6.5). Background information is usually derived from the general topic area in GALA (e.g. the Banking Crisis) and definitions from the specific aspect of the general topic area in GALA (e.g. de-regulation) but, as stated earlier, it is not always the case that you need to define things, so bear that in mind.

Figure 6.5 Updated generic essay template

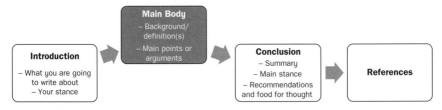

Let's look at further examples to make sure that you know how to structure your essay after applying GALA. Remember, the point of GALA is to deconstruct your essay question to give you a full understanding of what you are being asked to do. The added bonus of GALA is that when you combine the results of GALA with the generic essay template (Figure 6.5), the roadmap for your essay starts to take shape.

Example 2

Account for the rise of Fascism in 1930s Italy.

Apply the GALA template (Table 6.3).

Table 6.3 Applying GALA (Example 2)

Essay Question: *Account for the rise of Fascism in 1930s Italy.*

	Question Deconstruction
General topic area:	*Fascism*
Aspect of general topic to be addressed:	*rise of Fascism*
Limiting word(s):	*1930s Italy*
Action word(s):	*Account for*: to provide an explanation or reason for something.

Rewriting the essay question using the definition of 'account for' gives us:

> *Provide an explanation for the rise of Fascism in 1930s Italy.*

Once again, the outline of an essay structure becomes obvious: definition of Fascism, Fascism in 1930s Italy, an explanation for this rise. Fitting into our generic template, the headings for our structure become:

- Introduction
- Definition of Fascism
- Background: Fascism in 1930s Italy
- Why Fascism Rose in 1930s Italy
- Conclusion
- References

When it comes to your specific structure, you have options. You could place the definition of Fascism and some background information about the rise of Fascism in Italy as part of an extended Introduction. This is perfectly acceptable, although doing so is not without its problems (discussed in Chapter 7). Your structure would then become:

- Introduction
- Why Fascism Rose in 1930s Italy
- Conclusion
- References

Alternatively, you could combine a definition of fascism with basic background information on its rise in Italy under the generic heading, 'Background: Fascism and its Rise in 1930s Italy', giving another acceptable structure:

- Introduction
- Background: Fascism and its Rise in 1930s Italy

- Why Fascism Rose in 1930s Italy
- Conclusion
- References

Regardless, you are tweaking your structure from a position of knowledge. Importantly, you have a clear idea, based on a well-considered approach, of the topics that you need to address in order to answer the essay question.

One further point. The heading 'Why Fascism Rose in 1930s Italy' does not indicate that you will cover that topic in one paragraph. It is the focus of your essay and will require the bulk of your words. If you have three reasons why Fascism rose in 1930s Italy, then it is likely that you will have a number of paragraphs devoted to each point. (More on this when we tackle Step 4: Write the Main Body.)

Example 3

> Outline the theory of constraints and apply it to an aspect of health care. Discuss your findings.

Apply the GALA template (Table 6.4).

This example raises a number of points:

1 There is no limiting word. That's not a problem. Although many essay questions restrict the scope of a question in terms of, for example, geographical location or time frame, that is not the case here.

Table 6.4 Applying GALA (Example 3)

Essay Question: *Outline the theory of constraints and apply it to an aspect of health care. Discuss your findings.*

	Question Deconstruction
General topic area:	*theory of constraints*
Aspect of general topic to be addressed:	*health care*
Limiting word(s):	–
Action word(s):	*Outline*: give a summary/sketch of main points/general features only.
	Apply: show through the use of relevant examples.
	Discuss: to debate an issue in the round, i.e. from different perspectives, including pros and cons, for and against, advantages and disadvantages, and so coming to a balanced conclusion.

2   More than one action word is used. When that happens weight your answer
to the higher-level tasks. In order of simplest first, the three action words
(i.e. tasks) are *outline*, *apply*, and *discuss*. That is because *outline* is a basic
task, *apply* is an intermediate task, and *discuss* is an advanced task. This
means that you spend more time on the discussion part than the application
part, and more time on the application part than the outline part.

Reinterpreting the essay question in light of the definitions of the three action
words:

* Original question: *Outline the theory of constraints and apply it to an
aspect of health care. Discuss your findings.*
* Rewriting the essay question, inserting definitions: *Summarise the general
features of the theory of constraints and show an example of it in one
aspect of health care. Use your findings to debate the arguments for and
against the theory of constraints.*

Once again, the structure for your essay jumps off the page at you: summary of
the general features of the theory of constraints; application of theory to health
care example; evidence that supports using the theory of constraints; evidence
that argues against using the theory of constraints; and conclusion. Combining
this information with the generic essay template (i.e. Introduction, Background/
Definitions, Main Points/Arguments, Conclusion, and References), gives us:

* Introduction
* Theory of Constraints: General Features
* Applying the Theory of Constraints: Health Care Case Study
* Advantages of the Theory of Constraints
* Disadvantages of the Theory of Constraints
* Conclusion
* References

Note. There is no need for a separate Background section because the general
features of the theory of constraints becomes your Background section. We
could have renamed that section Background: The Theory of Constraints.

Example 4

> With reference to three paintings of your choice, describe the main character-
> istics of Impressionism.

Apply the GALA template (Table 6.5).
Rewriting essay question using definition of action word:

> With reference to three paintings of your choice, capture, in detail, the main
> characteristics of Impressionism.[1]

Table 6.5   Applying GALA (Example 4)

Essay Question: *With reference to three paintings of your choice, describe the main characteristics of Impressionism.*

	Question Deconstruction
General topic area:	*Impressionism*
Aspect of general topic to be addressed:	*main characteristics*
Limiting word(s):	*With reference to . . . three paintings*
Action word(s):	*Describe*: capture the main features of something or relate an event in detail.

Combining the generic essay template with the specific requirements of the essay question gives us the following essay structure:

- Introduction
- Background: Impressionism
- Painting 1
- Painting 2
- Painting 3
- Conclusion
- References

The Background section could set the scene by providing a basic definition of Impressionism and some historical sense of when Impressionism took off. It is when discussing the three paintings that the main characteristics of Impressionism would come to life. In reality, you would name the painting and the artists rather than give the bland, uninformative headings, 'Painting 1', etc. For example:

- Introduction
- Background: Impressionism
- Painting 1: *Nymphéas* by Claude Monet
- Painting 2: *Un bar aux Folies-Bergère* by Édouard Manet
- Painting 3: *Le déjeuner des canotiers* by Pierre-Auguste Renoir
- Conclusion
- References

Example 5

Evaluate the usefulness of social media as a marketing tool.

Table 6.6 Applying GALA (Example 5)

Essay Question: *Evaluate the usefulness of social media as a marketing tool.*

Question Deconstruction	
General topic area:	*social media*
Aspect of general topic to be addressed:	*usefulness*
Limiting word(s):	*marketing tool*
Action word(s):	*Evaluate*: Judge the worth – value – of something by appraising its benefits and limitations, using reliable sources as evidence.

Apply the GALA template (Table 6.6).

Rewriting essay question using definition of action word:

Judge the worth of social media as a marketing tool by appraising its benefits and limitations, using reliable sources as evidence.

Essay structure:

- Introduction
- Background: Social Media
- Benefits of Social Media as a Marketing Tool
- Limitations of Social Media as a Marketing Tool
- Conclusion
- References

Creating a roadmap allows you to see where you are going. The absence of one, on the other hand, can lead to uncertainty, no small amount of anxiety, and a dependence on guesswork. Be smart: plan ahead. The next step – Step 3 – shows you how to introduce your essay.

Summary of key points

- An essay is a journey. Like all journeys, planning is important. A roadmap, in the context of a university essay, forms the structure of your essay.
- The structure of your essay is, in turn, represented by headings.
- The generic structure of a university essay consists of Introduction, Main Body, Conclusion, and References. The Main Body can be further subdivided into Background Information and/or Definitions, followed by Main Points/ Arguments.
- The normal weighting, in terms of words, generally follows the 10:80:10 rule: 10 per cent for the Introduction, 80 per cent for the Main Body, and 10 per cent for the Conclusion, although there is scope for readjustment.
- To arrive at an essay structure that is tailored to a specific essay question involves a simple three-pronged approach: (1) apply GALA; (2) rewrite the essay question using action word definitions; and (3) embed the information from (1) and (2) into the generic essay template.
- It is normally a matter of personal choice whether or not you decide to retain your essay headings after you complete your essay. They helped guide *you* – so keeping them may also help guide your *marker*.

7 Step 3: Introduce your essay

Pre-stage
Introduce your essay

This chapter tells you how to write an Introduction and highlights the main elements that an introduction ought to contain. Prior to writing your Introduction, you should have assembled and read key literature sources and, where appropriate, arrived at a position/thesis that you intend to defend.

Pre-stage

Writing a university essay can be divided into five steps. The first two steps lay the groundwork for your essay, namely: (1) how to break down your essay question and, as a result of that process, (2) how to create a roadmap. These steps were covered in Chapters 5 and 6 respectively. The next step – Step 3 – kickstarts the writing process by showing you, through an example, how to introduce your essay:

Step 1: Deconstruct the essay question ✓
Step 2: Create a roadmap ✓
Step 3: Introduce your essay
Step 4: Write the Main Body
Step 5: Conclude your essay

Prior to writing your Introduction, you should have sought out the literature sources that you will use in support of the points or arguments that you will make in your essay. It therefore makes sense to have most of your reading material in front of you and, before you start your essay, all of it read (sorted and annotated if necessary). In that way, you will know who is saying what in relation to the focus of the essay question and so be better placed to form your own opinion, too. Remember, it is an academic essay that you are writing, so you need to show that you are well-read, that what you are reading is relevant to your essay, that it has credibility in the academic community, and that it is not out of date. In other words, your source material should reflect the 3 Rs highlighted at the start of Chapter 3 (Figure 3.1): that is, sources cited should be (reasonably) Recent, Relevant, and Reliable.

The idea of credible literature is crucial to adding academic weight to your essay. Too often students look to (academically) dubious web sources for information. In the first instance, search your university library for reliable sources. The books in your library do not appear by accident: they have been recommended by academics who are specialists in your field. Your module descriptor will also have a recommended reading list – look up the material that might be relevant to your essay. Similarly, you should check recommended internal and external university databases – such as JSTOR, Emerald, and ERIC – for key books, reports, journals, and conference papers. Google Scholar is also a quick way to access scholarly documents. You can type in either an author's name or a topic title in the search box, and even restrict entries according to particular years. Ending a query with the letters 'PDF' (e.g. First World War PDF) will give you PDF documents on your subject area.

 A common student mistake

A common mistake by students is to focus too much on questionable online sources. Your reference list should be constructed primarily from books, reports, journal papers, and conference proceedings (i.e. credible academic sources, whether online or in print).

Your literature sources need to be relevant to your essay and that, in turn, is determined by combining the structure you produced as a result of applying GALA with the generic essay template (Introduction, Background, Main Points/Arguments, Conclusion, References).

Let's look at an example from Chapter 6 (Example 1), where we used GALA to create a roadmap (i.e. essay structure) for the essay question, *Assess the part that de-regulation played in the 2008 banking crisis.* Applying GALA gave us Table 7.1.

We then incorporated the results of GALA into the generic essay template:

- Introduction
- Background/Definitions
- Main Points/Arguments
- Conclusion
- References

Table 7.1 Applying GALA

Essay Question: *Assess the part that de-regulation played in the 2008 banking crisis.*

	Question Deconstruction
General topic area?	*banking crisis*
Aspect of general topic to be addressed?	*de-regulation*
Limiting word(s)?	*2008*
Action word(s)?	*Assess:* Estimate the worth/value of something by weighing up the advantages and disadvantages or strengths and weaknesses or arguments for and against.

Combining the results of GALA with the generic essay template gave us the following structure:

- Introduction
- Background: The Banking Crisis
- Definition: De-regulation
- De-regulation to Blame for the Banking Crisis?
- The Banking Crisis: Other Factors?
- Conclusion
- References

It is now an easy matter to break down the literature needed to support the various parts of that essay. This follows naturally from the core subject headings (Table 7.2).

Once you know the topics that you need to read about (e.g. general literature on the banking crisis and literature that defines 'de-regulation'), your next step is to locate that literature. Look for it in trusted places: check your module reading list, the university library, internal and external academic databases, Google Scholar, etc. Be focused. Look for material that reflects your essay headings. As you collate the material, keep it in distinct piles – digital or physical – as shown in Figure 7.1.

You will have to go through a sifting process to form your structured piles of literature. Some of the books, chapters, papers, or reports that you read may initially appear to be related to your essay but, on closer reading, you may discover that is not the case. You will quickly learn to discard irrelevant material.

Table 7.2   Literature topics

Essay structure	Literature topics
Introduction	
The Banking Crisis	General literature on the banking crisis
Definition: De-regulation	Literature that defines 'de-regulation'
De-regulation to Blame for the Banking Crisis?	Literature that primarily supports the notion that de-regulation is to blame for the banking crisis
The Banking Crisis: Other Factors	Literature that blames, in part or whole, factors other than de-regulation for the banking crisis
Conclusion	
References	

Figure 7.1 Collate essay literature

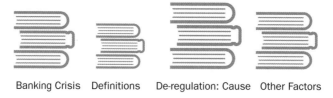

Banking Crisis   Definitions   De-regulation: Cause   Other Factors

For books, a brief look at the contents page and index will give you a clue as to the potential relevance of the material; for academic papers, read the abstract; and for reports, there is usually a summary (sometimes called a *synopsis*) that will outline what's in the report. Conclusions will also emphasise the stance adopted in learned articles. Even as you write your essay, it is likely that you will come across new material. That's fine. If you adopt the strategy outlined here, then you will know exactly what literature topics you need and where to fit them into your essay.

The huge advantages of acquiring, sorting, and reading core literature before you start your essay are as follows:

1   You will have an overview of the subject area as it relates to your essay.
2   You will have a good idea of the literature that you intend citing in the various parts of your essay.
3   Importantly, you ought to have arrived at an *informed opinion* on where you stand. For instance – related to the previous example – is the evidence pointing to de-regulation as the main cause of the banking crisis or are there other factors that need to be taken into account?

Not all university essays require you to take a stance; some essays, particularly some first-year undergraduate essays, only ask that you describe matters. But most university essays *do* expect you to adopt a position (also known as your *thesis*). You will see in the next section that your position/thesis is declared openly and unambiguously in your Introduction.

A word on word limit

As a general rule, the breakdown of your essay, in terms of the stipulated maximum word count, generally follows the 10:80:10 rule: 10 per cent of your words towards your Introduction, 80 per cent for your Main Body, and 10 per cent for your Conclusion. You can tweak it here and there but it is a good rough estimate. Your reference list is not included in your word count.

There is a caveat to the 10:80:10 rule, however. Allocating about 10 per cent of your available words to your Introduction works when your essay is in the region of 1,000 words; but, when you have a 2,000-word essay to complete, or even more, then your Introduction becomes too big and will just bore the reader and detract from your core essay. To illustrate this point, here's what 10 per cent of 1,000 words, 2,000 words, and 3,000 words look like, respectively:

10 per cent of 1,000 words (= 100 words)

Word word.

10 per cent of 2,000 words (= 200 words)

Word word.

10 per cent of 3,000 words (= 300 words)

Word word.

If you view your essay as a meal, then the Introduction is the appetiser: its purpose is to whet the reader's appetite. That can be done easily in no more than 100 words, give or take a few. Stuffing your guest with 200 or 300 *bon mots* may ruin the main meal. So, let's add a gentle caveat to the 10:80:10 rule: this rule applies provided we do not excessively exceed 100 words in our Introduction. The next section shows you how to introduce your essay.

Introduce your essay

Most students struggle to write a good Introduction. Very often they just end up repeating the essay question and that is because they haven't broken down the essay question, understood what is being asked of them, developed an appropriate structure, gathered and read the necessary literature beforehand, and worked out where they stand in relation to what others say. In short, they are still trying to figure out what the essay question means and how to respond to it. You can't start something effectively if you don't know where you're going.

Before you start to write your Introduction, you need to structure your essay. Once you do that, you can write your Introduction from a position of knowledge. You get the structure of your essay from deconstructing the essay question – and you do that by applying GALA, with particular focus on the meaning of the action word(s) in the essay question. It is the action word(s) that direct your tasks.

> **A common student mistake**
>
> A common mistake by students is to write their Introduction without understanding fully what they are being asked to write about (i.e. they have neither deconstructed the essay question nor worked out the structure of their essay). As a result, they are reduced to repeating the essay question in their Introduction.

Figure 7.2 Generic essay template

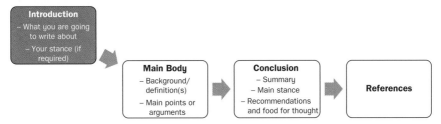

Chapter 6 provided an overall framework for your essay, reflecting a solid generic essay structure (see Figure 7.2). For an essay Introduction, two key parts were highlighted: the need to inform the reader of what you are going to write about and your own stance/position/thesis in relation to that topic. Where a university essay does not require critical commentary (e.g. the essay question simply asks you to describe something), then no stance is required.

The basic Introduction

From this template (Figure 7.2), it is clear that an Introduction should do two main things:

- identify what you are going to write about;
- state your stance.

But where do you get the information on what you are going to write about? Let's stick with the example from the essay question, *Assess the part that de-regulation played in the 2008 banking crisis*. As we saw, incorporating the results of GALA into the generic essay template gave us the following essay structure:

- Introduction
- **Background: The Banking Crisis**
- **Definition: De-regulation**

- **De-regulation to Blame for the Banking Crisis?**
- **The Banking Crisis: Other Factors?**
- Conclusion
- References

The parts (in **bold**) between the Introduction and the conclusion are what you are going to write about (if you were to produce that essay). We can now complete the first part of our Introduction, making sure to cover the items in the aforementioned list (Background: The Banking Crisis; Definition: De-regulation; De-regulation to Blame for the Banking Crisis?; and The Banking Crisis: Other Factors?):

> To understand the banking crisis, and the part played by de-regulation, it is necessary to provide some background information, define de-regulation, and examine explicitly the link between de-regulation and the banking crisis, including other contributing factors.

Next, we should state our stance. In the context of this essay, we need to decide if de-regulation was to blame for the banking crisis, in whole, part, or at all. Let's suppose we decide that it was the main reason, although there were other contributing factors. You can state your stance before or after you indicate what you are going to write about. Let's do it before:

> De-regulation was the primary cause of the 2008 banking crisis, although there were other contributing factors. To understand the banking crisis, and the part played by de-regulation, it is necessary to provide some background information, define de-regulation, and examine explicitly the link between de-regulation and the banking crisis, including the (lesser) impact of other contributing factors.

!   A common student mistake

Typically, students will refer to their essay in the Introduction with the words, 'This essay . . .', as in 'This essay will assess . . .'. There is no need to remind the reader that it is an essay: it is a redundant piece of information. You can assume that the reader is aware that they are reading an essay. It is what follows after, '**This essay will** . . .' that is important, so concentrate on that. For example, one could write:

> To understand the banking crisis, and the part played by de-regulation, this essay will provide some background information, define de-regulation . . .

Or we can instead replace the words 'this essay will' with the text in bold:

> To understand the banking crisis, and the part played by de-regulation, **it is necessary to** provide some background information, define de-regulation . . .

One criticism of giving away your position immediately is that you are starting your essay with a conclusion. In a way you are, but when you reiterate your conclusion at the end of your essay, you will do so from an informed position, thus providing *cyclical closure*. Cyclical closure is a useful literary trick, often used in debating circles: it signals that you have finished, but in a way that neatly dovetails with something you mentioned at the start of your journey.

The point of stating your stance in your Introduction is that you do not have time to take the reader on a mystery tour (essays, by their nature, are short). Your marker wants to know (1) what you think, and (2) why you think that. Addressing (1) immediately removes the guessing game, and possibility of drift on your part, and allows you and the marker to concentrate on (2). In effect, doing so concentrates the mind. Remember, in an essay, focus is your friend.

You might decide against stating your position in your Introduction. Perhaps your department or tutor prefers that you allow your position to unravel as you progress through your essay or perhaps it is your personal preference. In which case, good luck with keeping yourself and your reader on track. You can still follow the rest of the advice in this chapter on how to write an Introduction but this book assumes that you will declare your stance upfront.

Of course, to start with your stance, you need to have one, and that, in turn, requires that you have read the literature. If you read while you write, trying to locate relevant material, then you will begin with no predefined position and end up taking yourself, as well as your marker, on a mystery tour. That is not a tour that you want to take because there is a danger that neither you nor your marker will have a clear idea of where you are going. After that, it is an uphill struggle to get good marks.

A more informed Introduction

So far, only two sentences have been used in our sample Introduction: one to identify the student's stance and one to inform the reader of the structure of the essay. The sample Introduction could be improved further by preceding the student's position and roadmap (in whatever order) with some (brief) comment or contextual information that gently introduces the reader to the essay. One sentence should suffice – two at most. Here is an example (in **bold**):

> **The banking crisis in 2008 was the worst financial disaster since the Great Depression of the 1930s.** De-regulation was the primary cause of the 2008 banking crisis, although there were other contributing factors. To understand the banking crisis, and the part played by de-regulation, it is necessary to provide some background information, define de-regulation, and examine explicitly the link between de-regulation and the banking crisis, including the (lesser) impact of other contributing factors.

The Introduction that ticks all the boxes

If you want to add an academic feel to your Introduction, then insert one or two references. This lets your marker know immediately that you are well-read.

Stick to indirect referencing and leave quotations to the main body of your essay (see next section, 'To quote or not to quote?'). Using the previous Introduction format, the references should appear either in the first sentence (in your opening comment), in support of your stance, or both. Here is an example (the references are in **bold** so that you can see them):

> The banking crisis in 2008 was the worst financial disaster since the Great Depression of the 1930s **(Burlington, 2009; Aitken, 2012)**. De-regulation was the primary cause of the 2008 banking crisis, although there were other contributing factors **(Reardon, 2016)**. To understand the banking crisis, and the part played by de-regulation, it is necessary to provide some background information, define de-regulation, and examine explicitly the link between de-regulation and the banking crisis, including the (lesser) impact of other contributing factors.

This assumes that you have read the required literature prior to writing your essay. Also, don't overdo referencing in your Introduction – it can distract the reader and, besides, you want to keep your main sources back for when you really need them (i.e. in the body of your essay).

To quote or not to quote?

A word or two on trying to impress with a quotation: avoid using one in your Introduction except where the essay question quotes someone. It is much safer and simpler to keep to indirect referencing – see Chapter 3, 'He said, she said (in-text referencing)'– for the following reasons:

- There is a danger that the rest of your essay concentrates on the quotation rather than the essay question! It is rare that the content of a quotation coincides completely with the requirements imposed by an essay question
- Even where a quotation provides evidence of the importance of a topic, or supports your stance, unless it is self-explanatory, you may find yourself having to explain what it means and its relevance, thus drifting away from a focused Introduction.
- Finding the right quotation takes up valuable time. You want to crack on with your essay.
- If the quotation is too long, then it will eat into your word count. It will also annoy your marker.
- Keep your powder dry. Quotations should be an infrequent occurrence in an essay – use them judiciously. Bring them in at key points in the body of your essay when you really need them. For example, when you need to describe, explain, or critique someone's position, or as evidence to support your own view on something.

So, unless your quotation is *ready to hand*, *short*, *relevant*, and *self-explanatory* – a tall order in an Introduction – avoid the urge to quote someone in your Introduction.

Figure 7.3 Updated generic essay template

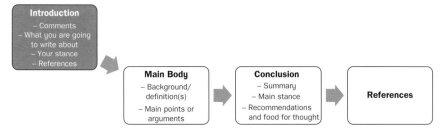

In summary, an effective Introduction should contain four key elements:

1   a contextual comment (one sentence, two at most);
2   what you are going to write about (one sentence, two at most);
3   your stance (one sentence);
4   one or two (indirect) references. Figure 7.2 is amended accordingly as Figure 7.3.

First impressions count, so make the effort!

Summary of key points

- Before you write your Introduction, read the literature relevant to your essay topic, and sort it into appropriate piles that reflect the essay structure derived from applying GALA.
- As a general rule, devote no more than 10 per cent of your word count to your Introduction, at least 80 per cent to the Main Body of your essay, and no more than 10 per cent to your Conclusion. Your reference list (or bibliography) does not form part of your word count.
- In relation to your Introduction, there is a caveat to the 10:80:10 rule: this rule applies provided you do not excessively exceed 100 words.
- A solid academic Introduction includes four elements: (1) an introductory contextual comment (one sentence, two at most); (2) what you are going to write about (one sentence, two at most); (3) your stance/position (one sentence); and (4) a reference or two. Elements (2) and (3) are interchangeable in terms of when they occur in your Introduction. If your essay is of the kind that does not require a position on your part (e.g. it is descriptive in nature), then element (3) is obviously omitted.
- Avoid using quotations in your Introduction unless you have one that is spot on and succinct or where the question makes use of a quotation.

8 Step 4: Write the Main Body

This chapter explains how to write the Main Body of your essay. Topics covered include: planning your word allocation; setting the scene; avoiding student drift; and the difference between description and critical commentary.

Pre-stage

After you have used GALA to deconstruct your essay question (Step 1), applied the generic essay template to create your roadmap (Step 2), and introduced your essay (Step 3), you should now be in a position to take the penultimate step, which is to write the Main Body of your essay:

Step 1:   Deconstruct the essay question ✓
Step 2:   Create a roadmap ✓
Step 3:   Introduce your essay ✓
Step 4:   Write the Main Body
Step 5:   Conclude your essay

As you can see from Figure 8.1, the Main Body of your essay has two core elements: (1) background information, including any terms that require to be defined; and (2) your main points or arguments. Generally, you should spend no more than 20 per cent (though, usually closer to 10 per cent) of your Main Body on background information/definitions and at least 80 per cent of your Main Body on meeting the core demands of the essay question reflected by the action word(s) used (e.g. *analyse*, *evaluate*, and *assess*). Let's remind ourselves of the 10:80:10 rule for the weighting of words in your finished essay (Figure 8.2) and how the division of words allocated for the Main Body follows the 10:80:10 rule.

Figure 8.1 Generic essay template

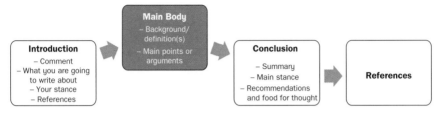

Figure 8.2 The 10:80:10 word allocation rule for the completed essay

Introduction (10%)   Main Body (80%)   Conclusion (10%)

Table 8.1 Division between background information/definitions and main points/arguments

Essay question	Background (1/5 at most)	Main points/arguments (4/5 +)
Assess the part that de-regulation played in the 2008 banking crisis.	Background on banking crisis; define de-regulation.	Part played by de-regulation.
Account for the rise of Fascism in 1930s Italy.	Background on 1930s Italy; define Fascism.	Reasons for the rise of Fascism in 1930s Italy.
Evaluate the usefulness of social media as a marketing tool.	Background on social media and marketing tools.	Usefulness of social media as a marketing tool.
Assess the contribution trade unions make to society.	Background on trade unions.	Contribution trade unions make to society.

Of the 80 per cent of words allocated for your Main Body, *no more than* one-fifth (20 per cent) of those will be for background/definitions and about four-fifths (80 per cent), *at least*, will be for your main points/arguments. Table 8.1 takes some sample essay questions and illustrates what this division means in practice.

There are those who will insist, perhaps quite reasonably, that background information, including definitions, is really part of your Introduction and that the Main Body should start with your main points/arguments. The problem with that interpretation is that students may be tempted to place their information in the opening paragraph. This would result in a very unwieldy and, more often than not, confusing Introduction, touching too many bases. It is more accurate to describe any required background information as a bridge that allows your reader to cross over from your Introduction to your main discussion without any difficulty.

Although the background information is a bridge between the Introduction and your essay proper, it makes sense to view it as a core element of the Main Body of your essay, for two reasons: first, markers start allocating serious marks after the introductory paragraph; secondly, students see background information/definitions as part of their essay proper – so much so that they are often guilty of spending too much time on background stuff and not enough time on addressing higher-level skills that they have been asked to perform (e.g. *assess* and *analyse*). This has the result that the latter is tacked on, almost as an afterthought, just before their Conclusion.

 A common student mistake

A common mistake by students, often lamented by markers, is that too many students get the weighting between their background information and their main discussion wrong, spending far too much time on the former and not enough time on the latter.

Sometimes an essay question will specifically ask you to provide background information. This usually happens when there are two or more action words in the essay question, with the first one a low-level action word that is used to ease you into your essay. Here are two examples:

- *Outline* the stages of Soft Systems Methodology and *assess* its contribution in the development of information systems.
- *Define* the philosophical terms 'empiricism' and 'rationalism' and *discuss* the central weaknesses of each theory.

In such cases, the person who set the question is trying to do you a favour by helpfully telling you what to write in your background information. More often than not, though, you will have to work this out for yourself. It's easy enough to do, as Table 8.1 illustrated.

This chapter will now show you how to confine your background information, including definitions, to one or two paragraphs – unless the weighting of the essay question dictates otherwise – and how to achieve the higher-level skills demanded of most university essays.

Write the Main Body

Set the scene: Background information

Let's suppose that you are studying for a degree in Educational Studies and that you have been given the following essay to write:

> *Consider the advantages and/or disadvantages of using group-work in student assignments.* [800 words +/− 10 per cent]

We will further assume that you have used GALA to deconstruct the essay question and that your position is that there are many advantages to using group-work for student assignments but that it doesn't come without its problems. Your roadmap looks like this (the text in **bold** is the Main Body of your essay):

- Introduction
- **Definition of group-work**
- **Benefits of group-work**
- **Problems with group-work**
- Conclusion and recommendations
- References

We'll also assume that you have written the Introduction.

Given the previous discussion on weighting, it make sense to start thinking about how many words you will apportion to each part of your essay, bearing in mind the 10:80:10 rule and the maximum word count allowed for the essay. With 800 words available (880 maximum, 720 minimum, if allowing for 10 per cent either way), we allocate 10 per cent of those to our Introduction (= 80 words), 10 per cent for our Conclusion[1] (= 80 words), and 80 per cent for our Main Body, including background information (= 640 words), giving:

- Introduction (approx. 80 words)
- **Definition of group-work** (share of 640 words)
- **Benefits of group-work** (share of 640 words)
- **Problems with group-work** (share of 640 words)
- Conclusion and recommendations (approx. 80 words)
- References

Of the 640 words for the Main Body of your essay, reserve no more than one-fifth for background information (one-fifth of 640 = 128) and no less than four-fifths for our main discussion (four-fifths of 640 = 512). The latter 512 words we will divide equally between the benefits of and problems with group-work (256 words each), giving:

- Introduction (approx. 80 words)
- **Definition of group-work** (*no more than* 128 words)
- **Benefits of group-work** (*no less than* 256 words)
- **Problems with group-work** (*no less than* 256 words)
- Conclusion and recommendations (approx. 80 words)
- References

This is a rough guide, of course, but a balanced one. And, remember, we still have an extra 80 words (exploiting the +/− 10 per cent) to be spread over our Introduction, Conclusion, or Main Body as we see fit. In addition, any words left over from background information can be split evenly between the benefits of and problems with group-work.

Now that we have our structure and word allocation sorted, let's now have a go at writing the background information for the essay, using no more than our allocated 128 words. The added benefit of allocating a maximum number of words to your background is that it stops you filling up your essay with background information. Suppose we decide to quote someone called Mullen who offers a definition of group-work.

> First attempt
>
> Mullen (2019, p.4) defines group-work as 'a vehicle for two or more people working collaboratively to achieve the same overall aim'.

It is not uncommon for tutors to witness a student write a paragraph that contains only a quotation (as in this example). Although it is evidence that the student has done some reading and (hopefully) that the student can cite sources properly, it sticks out like a sore thumb, but like all sore thumbs, not in a good way. A quotation on its own, though, is not background information. If something deserves a quote, then it deserves a comment too. Besides, you are also getting marks for showing that you understand what you are reading. In the context of a quotation, you do that by either explaining the quotation (to show that you know what it means) or by offering an opinion on the quotation itself, or part of it. Let's comment on part of the quotation:

> Second attempt
>
> Mullen (2019, p.4) defines group-work as 'a vehicle for two or more people working collaboratively to achieve the same overall aim'. The word 'vehicle' is deliberate and suggests that group-work does not just happen – it has to be designed carefully.

Now we are getting somewhere. The marker has more evidence that we can cite a source properly and, furthermore, that we can interpret sources, in this case by highlighting a key concept often overlooked in group-work: planning on the part of those who want to introduce group-work. However, there is still something missing. If you want to explain what something means, then give an example:

that is the clearest way of showing your marker that you *know* what you are writing about. In this case, our example should be on student assignments:

Third attempt

Mullen (2019, p.4) defines group-work as 'a vehicle for two or more people working collaboratively to achieve the same overall aim'. The word 'vehicle' is deliberate and suggests that group-work does not just happen – it has to be designed carefully. An example of group-work in education would be where a class of art students are broken into groups of no more than three students, with each group tasked with giving a presentation on the statement: 'Picasso was a genius, but not in the way you think'. The group would then agree amongst themselves on their roles to achieve that task and then plan the presentation accordingly.

Relative to the number of words that we have available, this is a solid background paragraph. It touches all the bases: (1) it cites a source;(2) the quotation is cited properly; (3) it comments on the quotation; and (4) it provides a relevant example to help illustrate the definition of group-work. And it has not exceeded the allocated 128 words – the paragraph is made up of 106 words.

Not all background sections in student essays are about defining things or quoting someone or are confined to one paragraph. Given the topic and the words available in the previous example, it made sense to define the key term 'group-work' and to do so in one paragraph. An alternative background paragraph could have focused on the pressures on educational institutions to reflect working practices 'in the real world' and, at the same time, alleviate increasing staff and student workloads; then again, those points could be left to the section on the benefits of group-work. Given more words to play with, we could have extended our background information to two paragraphs: one on defining group-work, the other on the pressures on universities to encourage group-work.

The Main Body proper

When it comes to the heart of the essay – the Main Body proper – there are two bugbears that particularly irk markers: (1) student drift, and (2) a tendency towards description when evidence of a higher-level skill is anticipated. Let's look at what these mean and how to avoid them.

Student drift

Student drift occurs when a student begins to stray from answering the essay question. It is a path that is very easy to take. One moment you are describing Wittgenstein's picture theory of language; the next, you happen to mention Wittgenstein's depression; and then, before you know it, you are discussing depression itself, when the essay ought to have focused on critiquing Wittgenstein's theory. This is normally the result of a lack of planning or a deliberate policy by students desperate to include everything that they have read about the essay subject ('I've read it, so you're getting it!'). The end product is the same: a failure to focus on the essay question and a loss of marks for irrelevance.

You are not getting marks for how quickly or 'naturally' you can write an essay, or for everything you know about a subject. You are getting marks for how well you answer a specific question. To do that, you must answer the question showing clear evidence of the expected skill level. In other words, relevance + appropriate skill level = high marks. The first part of that equation – *relevance* – is the opposite of student drift.

Hierarchical signposting is the key to avoiding student drift. Your first level of signposting occurs at an earlier stage when you deconstruct your essay question using GALA and incorporate the results of that into the generic essay template. The signposts for your essay are essentially your subheadings. If you wish, you can remove or retain them once you have completed your essay. Examples of signposting are shown in Table 8.2 (the Main Body proper subheadings are in **bold**).

There will be times when the Main Body proper may only have one signpost, as in:

- Introduction
- Background: Fascism and its Rise in 1930s Italy
- **Why Fascism Rose in 1930s Italy**
- Conclusion
- References

That's perfectly acceptable. This now leads us on to more detailed signposting – micro signposting within subheading(s). To do this, you create further subheadings for each point/issue you want to cover for the parts that form the core of your essay. For example, if the heart of your essay has the subheading, 'Why Fascism Rose in 1930s Italy', then your explanation might highlight the following issues:

Why Fascism Rose in 1930s Italy

- Italian Nationalism
- Corporate Economic System
- Mussolini and the Debecale of Individualism

To take another example, if the core of your answer is reflected in the two subheadings, 'Benefits of Group-work' and 'Problems with Group-work', then for each of these subheadings, you might decide to discuss the following issues:

Benefits of Group-work

- Benefits to Students
- Benefits to Tutors

Table 8.2 Examples of signposting to avoid student drift

Example 1	Example 2	Example 3	Example 4
Introduction	Introduction	Introduction	Introduction
Background: The Banking Crisis	Background: Impressionism	Background: Social Media	Definition of Group-work
Definition: De-regulation	**Painting 1: *Nymphéas* by Claude Monet**	**Benefits of Social Media as a Marketing Tool**	**Benefits of Group-work**
De-regulation to Blame for the Banking Crisis?	**Painting 2: *Un bar aux Folies Bergère* by Édouard Manet**	**Limitations of Social Media as a Marketing Tool**	**Problems with Group-work**
The Banking Crisis: Other Factors?	**Painting 3: *Le déjeuner des canotiers* by Pierre-Auguste Renoir**	Conclusion	Conclusion and Recommendations
Conclusion	Conclusion	References	References
References	References		

| Problems with Group-work

- Problems for Students
- Problems for Tutors

You continue drilling down the core subheadings until you achieve a level of granularity that allows you to identify single points. Collectively, these single points will cover the issues under each subheading. You can use a quick spider diagram to remind yourself of the points you want to make under each sub-heading. For example, for 'Benefits to Students' you might produce the spider-gram shown in Figure 8.3.

Figure 8.3 Example spidergram

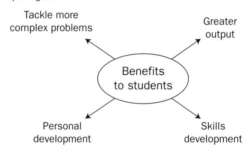

You would then know to write about four benefits of group-work to students: (1) that it would allow students the opportunity to tackle more complex problems than if they did the assignment themselves; (2) that students' collective output would be greater than if they did the assignment themselves; (3) that students would be able to develop group-work skills; and (4) that students would learn about themselves and how they react to working in a team. It's clear that point (3) requires further drilling to identify what skills are being developed, so you might want to list what those skills are (e.g. time management, communication skills, and role responsibility). You would then repeat that process for the other topics under each subheading: for 'Benefits to Tutors', sketch a spidergram and identify the points you want to make; do the same for 'Problems for Students' and 'Problems for Staff'.

The hierarchical structure for your essay could begin to look something like this:

- Introduction
  - **Definition of group-work**
  - **Benefits of group-work**
    - **Benefits to Students**
      - Tackle more complex problems
      - Greater output

- – Skills development
- – Personal development
  - ○ **Benefits to Staff**
  - ○ **Problems with group-work**
- Conclusion and recommendations
- References

A word of warning. Do not retain the lower-level headings: they will make your essay appear 'bitty' and superficial. If you do keep them, then you will end up with each lower-level heading having only one paragraph. The lower-level headings are there purely as reminders to you about the points you want to cover. If we take the previous example, then your main structure should still appear like this to you and your marker:

- Introduction
  - ○ **Definition of group-work**
  - ○ **Benefits of group-work**
  - ○ **Problems with group-work**
- Conclusion and recommendations
- References

Although your essay structure should appear obvious to anyone reading it, it is a matter of personal choice as to whether you wish to keep any headings at all in your final essay. The over-riding benefit of doing so is that your structure becomes crystal-clear to your audience. There is another less obvious benefit: if you precede the heading for your background information with the word 'Background', then it lets anyone reading it know that you are not wandering off track – they might assume that to be the case if they don't recognise it as background information! – but that you are instead providing this information for their benefit so that they can better understand what follows. Also, if you keep your headings, then there is no need to have one for your introduction or conclusion: it is plain when your essay begins and when it ends. A headed introduction becomes even more redundant when you have a title. A final (submitted) structure for the previous essay would look like this:

Group-work in Student Essays: Advantages and Disadvantages

- (Introduction)

- Background: What is group-work?

- Benefits of group-work

- Problems with group-work

- (Conclusion and recommendations)

- References

Obtaining this degree of detail is dependent on you deconstructing the essay question properly, fitting it into the generic essay structure (Introduction, Background, Main Points or Arguments, Conclusion, References), and then identifying the lower-level points you want to make. And all of that is dependent on you reading the appropriate literature and arriving at a position you intend to defend (unless it is a purely descriptive essay).

How you weight the elements within your Main Body proper is up to you. If you take a completely balanced view about your topic, then you might weigh up the issues evenly (e.g. 50 per cent of your words to the 'Benefits of Group-work', 50 per cent to the 'Problems with Group-work'). On the other hand, if you decide that the benefits of group-work outweigh the problems, then you might lean towards writing more on the benefits (e.g. 70 per cent to 'Benefits of Group-work' and 30 per cent to 'Problems with Group-work'). Normally, if you favour a particular position, then that is the one you write more about because it is the one you are defending/advancing and the more you write on it, the more convinced your reader should become. The amount you write on each identified point depends on how many words you have to play with. An 800-word essay means that you'll spend one or two sentences on some points, while other, more important points will merit a complete paragraph or two; a 2,000-word essay will allow more detailed discussion, and so on.

The benefits derived from introducing temporary sub-levels to your main essay structure now ought to be obvious: they keep you from drifting away from the essay question and, furthermore, help you identify the topics you want to cover and the points you want to make within each topic.

Description vs critical commentary

At this stage, you should have written the Background section, including any terms that require clarification, thereby setting the scene for the core of your essay. In addition, you should have a list of the points you want to cover and the literature you will be using for each point. You also ought to know how to write a paragraph in a student essay: basically, start each paragraph with a topic sentence and then write about that topic (see Chapter 1). A topic can stretch to more than one paragraph. Essentially, you will devote at least one paragraph to each meaningful point you want to make.

However, this is where serious marks are lost and won. You get high marks for showing clear evidence of the academic skill expected of you. This skill level is normally found in the action word(s) used in the essay question, examples of which are *assess, describe, discuss, explain*, and *evaluate*. Most university essays concentrate on the higher-level skills (i.e. the ones that demand evidence of critical commentary). Unfortunately, there is a tendency by many students to resort to description as their default position irrespective of any higher-level action word appearing in the essay question. Recalling the discussion in Chapter 4, action words can be divided into three broad classes: basic, intermediate, and advanced. Table 8.3 provides examples of action words under each classification.

Table 8.3 Examples of basic, intermediate, and advanced action words

Basic	Intermediate	Advanced
Annotate	Clarify	Analyse
Define	Consider	Assess
List	Describe	Discuss
Outline	Illustrate	Evaluate

If an essay only asks you to perform a task that is basic, then it is more likely to be an early first-year undergraduate essay. Basic action words can also be used as the first part of a double-barrelled question where the second action word is at intermediate or advanced level (e.g. **Define** *what you understand by the term post-modernism and **assess** its place in the history of modern art*). In such cases, basic action words help shape the content of the background section. Description occurs in every essay, and necessarily so. Even when you are asked to complete a higher-level task, you must first describe what you intend assessing, evaluating, etc. The trick is not to get carried away with the former to the detriment of the latter.

Describe is an intermediate action word, meaning 'capture the main features of something or relate an event in detail'. Here is an example of two paragraphs that describe something, in this case something called Soft Systems Methodology:

Soft Systems Methodology (SSM) was developed to bring clarity to problem situations where the system to be developed was not well understood (Checkland, 1981). It does this through a seven-stage process (see Diagram 1). Imagine that a university's policy on plagiarism is in need of clarity and rigour. The first stage of SSM would be to *determine the situation*. This may involve interviewing various stakeholders (e.g. managers, tutors, and students). The second stage is where the situation found is *expressed* diagrammatically using 'rich pictures' (i.e. unstructured but informative doodles that anyone can understand). The third stage requires key terms to be *defined* using CATWOE: **C**ustomers (e.g. students), **A**ctors (e.g. tutors), the desired **T**ransformation (i.e. a fair and reliable plagiarism policy), stakeholder **W**orld views (e.g. views of staff and students), the **O**wners of the system (e.g. Head of School), as well as information about the **E**nvironment (e.g. campus and online).

Once the system under investigation is better understood, the final stages of SSM are implemented: stage four – a *model* of the current messy system is built; stage five – this model is *compared* to what happens elsewhere (e.g. against plagiarism models used by other universities); stage six – specific *desirable changes* are then identified (e.g. definition of what constitutes plagiarism and what counts as evidence); finally, stage seven – a list of *actions* are recommended. In effect, SSM is a person-focused front-end process used to get to grips with a problem situation before any hard or technical solution is decided. Hence the name 'soft'.

This description is good on a number of levels. It cites a source, gives easy-to-understand descriptions, uses examples to enhance those descriptions, makes use of a diagram, and neatly summarises the essence of SSM at the end. You should try and replicate some of these features when you describe something. In particular, recognise the importance of writing in a way that allows a non-specialist to follow your narrative and the use of examples to show that you understand what you are writing about. Also note that each paragraph has a simple structure: an early topic sentence + narrative on that topic.

A common student mistake

Where a higher-level skill is asked for in an essay question, a common mistake by students is to focus on copious description to the detriment of in-depth evaluation, only offering (often unsupported) opinion towards the end of their essay.

On the negative side, there is no evidence of higher-level skills in the previous descriptions. In other words, there is no critical commentary on SSM. If the essay question had been, 'Critically evaluate the usefulness of Soft Systems Methodology (SSM) in the development of ill-defined problems', then the paragraphs (together with a diagram) only set the scene and are better placed in the background section. An example of a paragraph that illustrates critical commentary is the following:

SSM is not without its limitations. In the first instance, for those unfamiliar with SSM it can appear woolly and ill-defined (Castle, 2017; Anderson, 2019). For example, it does not provide clear guidance on how to *determine the situation* (stage one): it assumes that you have the skills to gather information from key stakeholders. Similarly, leaving the facilitator to draw a rich picture of the current system (stage two), including complex issues, without detailed advice on how to construct these pictures, is a tall order. Most people are nervous about displaying their drawing skills. To do so without step-by-step instruction is not helpful. Even the W in CATWOE is unnecessarily strange: it stands for Weltanschauung, which is interpreted to mean *world view*. This is not a term that the average workforce will ordinarily come across, much less understand. Furthermore, Riley (2018, p. 12) pointedly asks: 'How do you build this model?' (stage four). He has a point. For example, what tools are available to build this model and where do you learn about these tools? Clearly, SSM is vulnerable to the charge of vagueness.

The student may then go on to offer critical commentary on different aspects of SSM (perhaps derived from a spidergram), devoting a paragraph or two to each point:

- Another criticism of SSM is that it assumes that workplaces are models of democracy, where all stakeholder views are expressed freely . . .
- Even if views are openly given, SSM may falter at the first hurdle if these views are not captured in full or if the problem is defined too narrowly . . .
- This leads on to a further issue: SSM relies too heavily on the expertise of the facilitator . . .
- Lastly, the notion implicit in SSM, that organisations will spend time, and money, on a 'soft' investigation of the 'problem situation', rather than on finding a 'hard' solution, is naive . . .

Although SSM is a real methodology, these criticisms, including the references, are invented for illustrative purposes only (the author considers SSM to be a simple and clever way to unpick complex problems), which leads us on to a salient matter: it is not important that your marker agrees with any position you favour, only that you can support your points with reasoned argument and pertinent sources.

There is another matter that requires clarification. In the world of academia, critical commentary does not mean that you always say bad things about something. In academia, critical commentary has a wider interpretation: it means that you can either highlight the bad things about something or the good things about something, or both, depending on the essay question. For instance, if you are asked to critically evaluate something, then you are being asked to judge the worth – or value – of something by appraising its benefits and limitations (using reliable sources as evidence). So, for example, the essay question, 'Critically evaluate the usefulness of Soft Systems Methodology (SSM) in the development of ill-defined problems', means that the student would have to judge the worth of SSM by appraising its benefits as well as its limitations. This student might decide to include a number of points in support of SSM before coming to a conclusion about its worth.

An example of a critical commentary that is positive in nature is as follows:

Understanding the problem-situation is a major benefit of SSM. Too often systems analysts focus their efforts on finding a hard, technical solution before they understand what the problem is, and this can result in expensive software-based solutions that are over-budget, late, and fail to meet user requirements (Wright, 2017; Black, 2018; Young, 2019). The over-riding advantage of SSM is that it makes time to ascertain who thinks what about the current situation, who has ownership, what it is they think they have ownership of, where they think are areas of conflict/failure, and it seeks opinion on how similar systems operate in other organisations. It is this emphasis on human issues that allows SSM to unravel a complex, messy problem and set the organisation on course to develop a new, improved system that meets user requirements.

The student may then go on to make other points in support of SSM, allocating a paragraph or two to each point:

* The fact that SSM is a non-technical process makes it easy for organisations to use . . .
* SSM is not without structure . . .
* Case studies show conclusively the advantages of SSM . . .

It should become apparent that there is a formula to applying **critical** commentary (cc), which is:

> **cc** = Describe something + [make a point about that something + support with evidence]^{Repeat}

The description could occur en bloc as background information (e.g. description of SSM), with the critical commentary appearing in the main essay proper, after the background information. Your evidence will be a combination of reasoned argument and other sources. You can also combine a description + point + evidence all in the one paragraph, even as early as the background information. For example:

> Roberts (2008, p. 64) defines e-Learning as 'the use of digital media to enhance understanding'. While this definition is commendably brief, it lacks clarity. Under this definition, anything that is digital would count as e-Learning. For example, newspapers that are online would count as e-Learning (one would get an understanding of the current issues in the news), as would websites that sold merchandise (one would get an understanding of items for sale and prices). Any definition of e-Learning ought to emphasise the primary environment where e-Learning normally resides (i.e. education) and give some examples of e-Learning to set the parameters. Roberts himself would have enhanced an understanding of e-Learning if he had defined it thus: 'E-Learning is the use of digital media in an educational environment to facilitate learning, examples of which are online referencing software, blogs on essay-writing, and virtual learning environments.'

Irrespective of whether you give evidence of using your critical faculties over one paragraph or more, with the description separate from the main commentary, or in the same paragraph, or a mixture of both, the equation for doing so remains the same: critical commentary = description + opinion + supporting evidence.

Title or no title?

Should you give your essay a title? Sometimes your essay-setter will allocate the title to you, in which case you should follow the instructions given. If you have not been given a title, however, then you are not normally required to include a title. But the main rationale for having one is simple: it immediately identifies the essay topic. Having a title is a good habit to get into because it is not only a helpful signpost to the reader, it also concentrates your mind and provides early evidence, albeit in a small way, that you can interpret and condense information.

Creating a title is easy. The quickest and simplest way is to ignore any action words in the essay question (such as *identify, assess,* and *describe*) and extract the title from the remaining text, in whole or part. If you include action words in the title, then it is more than likely that you will fall into the trap of merely repeating the essay question, making your title clunky and unwieldy; removing the action word(s) brings focus and clarity to the subject area (as well as reducing the word count). The following essay question illustrates this by showing two titles, one with the action word included, and one without. The second title has the benefit of brevity and focus.

Essay question: Assess the part that de-regulation played in the 2008 banking crisis.

Title 1: *An Assessment of the Part that De-regulation Played in the 2008 Banking Crisis*

Title 2: *De-regulation and the 2008 Banking Crisis*

Notice in this example that the title has been italicised and partially capitalised. Some students capitalise the whole title and make it bold, as in:

AN ASSESSMENT OF THE PART THAT DE-REGULATION PLAYED IN THE 2008 BANKING CRISIS

or

DE-REGULATION AND THE 2008 BANKING CRISIS

The result is a title that is just too shouty: **YOOHOO! OVER HERE! LOOK AT ME!!** Italics coupled with partial capital letters for the start of the larger words and not the smaller connecting words (*the, and, or, with,* etc.) creates a gentler, less garish title. It is permissible to slightly elevate your title from the rest of the essay by increasing its text size by one point.

Here are some other examples where we drop the action word and concentrate on using the remaining text in whole or part (initial action words in ***bold italics***):

Essay question: ***Account for*** *the rise of Fascism in 1930s Italy.*

Title: *The Rise of Fascism in 1930s Italy.*

Essay question: ***Evaluate*** *the usefulness of social media as a marketing tool.*

Title: *Social Media as a Marketing Tool.*

Essay question: ***Analyse*** *the contribution trade unions make to society.*

Title: *Trade Unions and their Contribution to Society.*

Another word of caution. Don't try and reinterpret the essay question or introduce a question mark: there is a danger that you might interpret wrongly or ask the wrong question!

Some might advise you to write a title once you have completed your essay. None of the example titles here depend on the student completing the essay. The reason for that is because any action words in the essay were set aside and that, in turn, made it easy to produce a title that focused purely on the essay topic and not on what we were going to do with the topic or what our slant on the topic was going to be. Your Introduction does that job quick enough anyway. You may also come across other advice that your title should be catchy, include keywords, adopt the right tone, avoid colloquialisms, and so on. Don't tie yourself in knots trying to meet a list of tick-box criteria. The best advice is to keep it simple and short. The approach just seen helps you to do just that.

What you should take away from this chapter is not a strict adherence to any rules (e.g. that you need to use 100 words for your Introduction; if you can do it in 70 words, then fine), or that your Background must form a fifth of the words you have allocated to your Main Body, or that you must retain subheadings or have a title. Instead, you should take away an appreciation of the general shape of what a university essay looks like, the importance of structure and planning to avoid student drift, and how to up your game from merely describing something to providing critical commentary, all with the objective of answering a specific essay question.

Summary of key points

- Plan your word allocation before you start writing. To start with, allocate at least 80 per cent of your words to the Main Body of your essay, which includes background information and the Main Body proper, with the weighting overwhelmingly towards the latter. Spend no more than 10 per cent of your words on your Introduction – provided that this does not excessively exceed 100 words – and no more than 10 per cent of your words on your Conclusion.
- Background information sets the scene for the reader, providing a context for the core of the essay. It is also an opportunity to clarify any terms that are used later in the essay.
- Student drift occurs when students begin to stray from answering the question. Hierarchical signposting is the key to avoiding student drift.
- Description, an intermediate skill, is the default position for many students. Most university essays demand evidence of a higher-level skill, such as the ability to assess, analyse, or evaluate (i.e. evidence of critical commentary).
- The process for providing evidence of **c**ritical **c**ommentary is captured in the formula:
  cc = describe something + [make a point about that something + support with evidence][Repeat].
- A title is normally optional, but it is easy to do and can be a useful signpost for the reader.

9 Step 5: Conclude your essay

Pre-stage
Conclude your essay

This chapter will show you how to develop your Conclusion.

Pre-stage

You have now reached the final stage of your essay, Step 5. You are now about to conclude your essay:

Step 1: Deconstruct the essay question ✓
Step 2: Create a roadmap ✓
Step 3: Introduce your essay ✓
Step 4: Write the Main Body ✓
Step 5: Conclude your essay

At this stage, you have made the effort: (1) to understand the essay question (using GALA); (2) to develop an appropriate structure; (3) to write a solid Introduction; and (4) to provide contextual background information and answer the essay question, showing evidence of the expected skill level. All of this you will have supported with properly cited sources coupled with a comprehensive reference list. You may feel that you have done all the hard work and so be tempted to rush your Conclusion. That would be a mistake. Just as first impressions count, so do final partings. Your Conclusion is not something that you want to treat lightly. It has an important part to play in your essay, which is best encapsulated by the term *cyclical closure*.

Cyclical closure basically involves reminding the reader what you wrote about. If you recall from Chapter 6, a university essay, stripped to its bare essentials, comprises an Introduction, a Main Body, and a Conclusion, reproduced here as Figure 9.1.

Figure 9.1 Generic essay template: Back to basics

Figure 9.2 Generic essay template

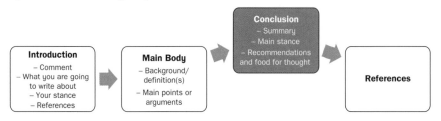

However, Figure 9.1 is an over-simplification of the essay process. It served a particular purpose in Chapter 6: to encourage an appreciation of the core functions of an Introduction, a Main Body, and a Conclusion. But just as we found out that an Introduction can be broken down further, and that the Main Body consists of a number of tasks, so it is with the Conclusion. In particular, cyclical closure is a three-pronged activity (Figure 9.2):

1 Summarising your essay.
2 Reiterating your main stance.
3 Leaving the reader with recommendations or food for thought.

Each of these concluding tasks is typically covered in one final paragraph. In terms of apportioning words to your Conclusion, following the 10:80:10 rule, you could spend up to 10 per cent of your words on your Conclusion. If your concluding paragraph is becoming too big, then of course split it in two. Given the three tasks that you have to complete, your Conclusion will normally be longer than your Introduction.

Importantly, a Conclusion is not the place to start a new discussion or introduce new evidence. You have done all your talking. Your marker is now expecting you to present your essay, all boxed up in a neat bow. Don't go opening other boxes. Particularly ones labelled 'Pandora'!

It's now time to learn how to write a Conclusion.

Conclude your essay

Of the three main activities that normally form a Conclusion – summary, main stance, recommendations/food for thought – two of these are compulsory: summarising your main points and a statement reinforcing your stance.[1] If the essay question asks that you make recommendations or discuss the implications of your findings, then not only are recommendations/implications to be included in your Conclusion but they will appear as a discussion point in the Main Body of your essay. You always have the option of ending with *food for thought* (i.e. an interesting observation on the implications of your essay or just a parting witticism).

One other matter needs to be raised on the content of your Conclusion. It may be that at the start of your essay, you decided against, for whatever reason, stating your position. In which case, you are not *restating* your position in your Conclusion but instead are allowing it to emerge logically from your discussion points. You have more work to do to show that your position follows as a result of your findings because you will need to make the connection between the points you made in your Main Body and what you conclude as a result of those points. If, on the other hand, you state your position at the start of your essay, then the points you make in the Main Body of your essay are making the case for your stance, which means that the connection between your position and your evidence has been made before you reach the final part of your essay.

This brings into sharp focus the meaning of the word 'conclusion'. A conclusion can be interpreted in two ways. It can be viewed as the final part of something (e.g. 'our journey came to a conclusion at Dover'). It can also be a position that has been arrived at as a result of reasoning and/or experience (e.g. 'I have come to the conclusion, after several blisters and much pain, that walking any distance of note requires proper footwear'). In the context of your essay, if you have already stated your position in your Introduction, then view your Conclusion simply as the final part of your essay (covering the three activities listed above); if you did not state your position in your Introduction, then you need to view your Conclusion as both the last part of your essay *and* as the place where you finally reveal the import of your reasoning.

In the following worked example, we will assume that the student's position has been stated at the start of the essay.

The basic Conclusion

You already know how to interpret an essay question that uses the action word 'assess' (e.g. *Assess the part that de-regulation played in the 2008 banking crisis*). Exploiting that experience, we'll explore the construction of a Conclusion for the essay question, *Assess the contribution trade unions make to society*. Let's suppose that the student makes a number of attempts at completing the Conclusion.

First attempt

It is clear that trade unions make a significant contribution to society. Through the principle of collective bargaining, trade unions improve employee standards in the workplace, including health and safety standards, skills development, wages, fair treatment, and improved working conditions, and, not least, are also at the forefront of equality, ensuring that organisations adhere to the Equality Act 2010. Nonetheless, as highlighted earlier, the beneficiaries are those in work; those out of work remain, by and large, unrepresented.

This conclusion would gain pass marks. It summarises the main points in the essay and restates the student's position (namely, that trade unions make a significant contribution to society). Note that your position can occur before or after you summarise the main points in your essay. Indeed, in this example, the student's position opens the concluding paragraph (in **bold**):

> **It is clear that trade unions make a significant contribution to society.** Through the principle of collective bargaining, trade unions improve employee standards in the workplace, including health and safety standards, skills development, wages, fair treatment, and improved working conditions, and, not least, are also at the forefront of equality, ensuring that organisations adhere to the Equality Act 2010. Nonetheless, as highlighted earlier, the beneficiaries are those in work; those out of work remain, by and large, unrepresented.

Don't think up your summary from scratch. You get your summary from the main discussion points in your essay. For instance, let's assume further that after deconstructing the essay question, the student produced the following roadmap, bearing in mind that 'assess' means to examine the strengths and weaknesses of something:

- Introduction
- Background: Facts and Figures
- The Benefits of Trade Unions
- The Problem with Trade Unions
- Conclusion
- References

Let's also assume that under 'The Benefits of Trade Unions', there was another level of headings. These (temporary) lower-level headings acted as reminders of the points to be covered:

- The Benefits of Trade Unions
    - Health and Safety
    - Skills Development
    - Wages
    - Improved Working Conditions
    - Opportunity for All

We will also assume that there were several minor criticisms of trade unions but that the main concern was that those not in the workplace lacked someone to stand up for them. It is from the content of the subheadings, if not the subheadings themselves, where the student will get the summary points on the contribution of trade unions to society. If you wish, for freshness, when it comes to your own Conclusion, you can rephrase some of your points – but do not introduce new points. For example, rephrasing a point, 'Opportunity for All' was really about trade unions making sure that organisations adhered to the Equality Act 2010.

A more informed Conclusion

Not all essays give you the opportunity to make recommendations within your Conclusion but where they do so, you should exploit it. The previous student's essay Conclusion pinpointed a problem with trade unions: that they only speak up for those in employment. An obvious recommendation is that trade unions should make more of an effort to speak up for the unemployed, beginning with letting them join a trade union at no cost. This results in an enhanced second attempt at writing the Conclusion. The new part added is in **bold**:

> It is clear that trade unions make a significant contribution to society. Through the principle of collective bargaining, trade unions improve employee standards in the workplace, including health and safety standards, skills development, wages, fair treatment, and improved working conditions and, not least, are also at the forefront of equality, ensuring that organisations adhere to the Equality Act 2010. Nonetheless, as highlighted earlier, the beneficiaries are those in work; those out of work remain, by and large, unrepresented. **Trade unions should make every effort to address this anomaly at no charge to the unemployed.**

This Conclusion now has the merit of: reaffirming the student's stance to remove any doubt; neatly summarising the essay's main discussion points; and offering a way forward on a contentious issue.

A Conclusion that ticks all the boxes

There are a number of linguistic tricks that allow you to finish with panache. Your final sentence can either (1) make a reference to a comment made in your Introduction (this option reinforces cyclical closure – a technique that is very popular in debating circles), or (2) make a parting observation/comment or witticism. Option (2) falls under the category of 'food for thought'. Suppose the student in the example chose option (2), highlighted in **bold**:

> It is clear that trade unions make a significant contribution to society. Through the principle of collective bargaining, trade unions improve employee standards in the workplace, including health and safety standards, skills development, wages, fair treatment, and improved working conditions and, not least, are also at the forefront of equality, ensuring that organisations adhere to the Equality Act 2010. Nonetheless, as highlighted earlier, the

> beneficiaries are those in work; those out of work remain, by and large, unrepresented. Trade unions should make every effort to address this anomaly at no charge to the unemployed. **After all, if society means anything at all, it means we should all be standing shoulder to shoulder – and that means everyone.**

We now have a well-rounded Conclusion, one that starts with our position, summarises the points that support that position, offers the way ahead, and ends with a relevant parting observation.

To quote or not to quote?

In regard to your Introduction, try and avoid using a quotation. When it comes to your Conclusion, however, that advice changes. A quotation in your Conclusion can have *impact*. However, it must be a short quotation, one that requires no explanation. Furthermore, it should not be one that introduces new evidence. So how *do* you use a quotation in your Conclusion? The best place to use it is in your last sentence, as 'food for thought'. It should flow naturally from the sentence that occurs immediately before the quotation. In effect, the quotation adds weight to what comes before it. In the previous example, imagine that someone called Hogarth had written: 'If society means anything at all, it means we should all be standing shoulder to shoulder – and that means everyone.' Then the Conclusion could have been completed thus:

> It is clear that trade unions make a significant contribution to society. Through the principle of collective bargaining, trade unions improve employee standards in the workplace, including health and safety standards, skills development, wages, fair treatment, and improved working conditions and, not least, are also at the forefront of equality, ensuring that organisations adhere to the Equality Act 2010. Nonetheless, as highlighted earlier, the beneficiaries of a trade union are those in work; those out of work remain, by and large, unrepresented. Trade unions should make every effort to address this anomaly at no charge to the unemployed. After all, **as Hogarth (2019) observed:** 'If society means anything at all, it means we should all be standing shoulder to shoulder – and that means everyone.'

You can see that the last sentence, wherein the quotation appears, acts as a parting observation, adding weight to the penultimate sentence, *Trade unions should make every effort to address this anomaly at no charge to the unemployed.*

Although your essay structure should be obvious to anyone reading it, it is a matter of personal choice or your university's essay-writing style guide as to whether you retain the headings in your final essay. The over-riding benefit of doing so is that your structure becomes crystal-clear to your audience. There is another less obvious benefit: if you precede the heading for your background information with the word 'Background', then it lets anyone reading it know that you are not wandering off track – they might assume that to be the case if they don't recognise it as background information – but that you are providing this information for their benefit so that they can better understand what follows. Also, if you keep your headings, then there is no need to have one for your Introduction or one for your Conclusion: it is clear where your essay begins and where it ends. A headed Introduction becomes even more redundant when you give your essay a title. For example, the final (submitted) structure for the essay could appear as follows:

The Contribution of Trade Unions to Society

- (Introduction)
- Background: Facts and Figures
- The Benefits of Trade Unions
- The Problem with Trade Unions
- (Conclusion)
- References

And so endeth your essay!

Summary of key points

- This chapter has taken you through the content of a Conclusion, from summarising the main points in the body of your essay, to reaffirming your main stance, to making recommendations and/or a parting observation/comment, as well as on how to use a quotation in your Conclusion.
- Your Conclusion is normally covered in one paragraph, two at most.
- The Conclusion consists of three activities: (1) a restatement of your stance; (2) a summary of your main points; and (3) either recommendations on the way forward or 'food for thought', or both. This is called *cyclical closure*.
- 'Food for thought' can either be a parting observation/comment or a witticism, or both.
- You can use a quotation in your Conclusion but make it short, relevant, self-explanatory, follow from the preceding sentence, and the last thing that you write.

Part 3

Learning from experience

10 Feedback

This chapter discusses the nature of formal feedback, what constitutes useful feedback, the importance of exploiting feedforward information, and how to respond to formal feedback.

Feedback (and feedforward)

Formal feedback

Formal feedback is normally associated with tutor commentary on graded assignments that contribute towards a module mark. The purpose of formal feedback is to highlight strengths and weaknesses with a view to informing future submissions.

Feedback is therefore about *learning*. It is not simply a justification of why you got a particular mark. More than that, it is an explanation of what went well in your essay and what didn't go so well. It is an opportunity for you to *understand* what you did that justified an E grade, or equivalent, and, equally important, what you did that justified an A grade, thereby allowing you to replicate what works and to remedy what doesn't. Such an activity is called *learning*, and is central to what it means to be a student.

Accordingly, you ought to approach feedback in a spirit of engagement, with a willingness to gain from the knowledge of those who are judging your work. There is no point in getting upset about feedback that is less than complimentary. Strange as it may seem, a bad mark early in your academic life may do you more good in the long run than a string of good marks, providing that you learn from the experience. Students who do well early in academia sometimes do not see the need to analyse why their essays are meritorious and when they later encounter more difficult essay questions (e.g. at Hons. level), they

Figure 10.1 Feedback standards: The 5 Cs

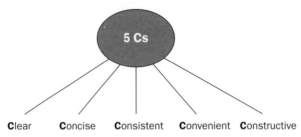

may not have the same wherewithal to cope as the student who has had to take corrective action after receiving a disappointing mark.

Formal feedback can be either written or verbal. Written formal feedback is the norm, traditionally coming in the shape of annotated notes in an essay but more commonly appearing in a standard or pro forma departmental feedback form. Written feedback also tends to be placed online for students to view and download. Formal verbal feedback usually occurs in one-to-one meetings between tutor and student to discuss a graded assignment and the formal written feedback. These meetings provide the opportunity to explore the rationale behind a mark as well as lessons to be learned.

Formal feedback, to be of any value to students, ought to meet certain criteria: it should be clear, concise, consistent, convenient, and constructive. Figure 10.1 captures these standards under the banner of the 5 Cs.

1 *Clear*: Feedback should be communicated using simple, unambiguous language, and preferably structured to reflect marking criteria used and linked to relevant learning outcomes. If the feedback is not clear to you, then all the other criteria that constitute good feedback (i.e. that it should be concise, consistent, convenient, and constructive) become irrelevant. If you do not understand your feedback, then you should arrange to speak to your marker with a view to seeking clarification.

2 *Concise*: Feedback ought to provide information in as few words as is necessary. A long-winded narrative is less memorable to students (who may also struggle to interpret and pick out salient points) than a headed or bullet-point list highlighting key issues for reflection. If your feedback is not concise, then you can raise this issue with your student representative for discussion at the next student–staff meeting or, better still, ask your marker to pick out the main points. Then again, some students welcome lengthy responses. In general, however, feedback that is direct and to the point is preferred.

3 *Consistent*: Feedback should be applied consistently throughout a programme. One way to facilitate consistency is through the use of a pro forma (standard feedback) form containing structured headings as well as definitions and explanations of terms used. Generic marking schemes can be embedded into a feedback pro forma document. This will help to ensure that

standards are maintained within and across departments and may also help combat claims of personal bias. As a matter of course, departments ought to be reviewing their feedback systems for consistency and effectiveness as part of an internal review process. Students expect feedback to be consistent in terms of timing and content. For students, lack of consistency would be a matter of concern. If your feedback is inconsistent, varying from one module to the next, or even within the same module, then this needs to be addressed. Your student representative is one port of call; another is the department administrator for your course. Importantly, you are not raising a complaint against a marker – you are simply highlighting an area for improvement.

4   *Convenient*: To be of use, feedback needs to be provided in a timely fashion, using a suitable method at a suitable place. Central to the concept of feedback is the notion that students can use the information to better prepare for the next assignment. Feedback that is late is worse than useless. Feedback also needs to be easily accessible for students (e.g. downloadable online). Importantly, students need to be informed when and how feedback operates in their programme. If this criterion is not met, then you can either ask your student representative to raise your concern at the next student–staff meeting, or you can contact the departmental administrator for your course.

5   *Constructive*: Feedback should be about what went well and what didn't go so well, with advice on the way forward. However, don't expect the marker to give you the answer. It is more important to understand how you arrived at your answer, what your marker thinks of your attempt, and how you could build on that understanding for future submissions. The tips on how to improve your performance may also direct you to an academic development unit or student support services, where you can seek additional support on specific issues (e.g. referencing, writing skills, and critiquing). This is called *constructive feedback*. Feedback that is wholly negative, without words of advice, is destructive feedback and offers very little in the way of learning points.

Informal feedback

Informal feedback is feedback that does not go through the formal departmental channels but that happens in everyday scenarios. Examples include meetings with your tutor prior to submission of your work, seminar discussions, Turnitin reports, lectures, advice from peers, and even self-reflection. Informal feedback is therefore not as structured and obvious as a formal feedback form and so it can be difficult to pick up the messages that others are giving you. One other major difference between informal and formal feedback is that formal feedback occurs after you receive your mark, whereas much informal feedback can, and indeed often does, occur before you submit your essay for marking.

Feedforward

Where informal and formal feedback are constructive (i.e. tell you where you went wrong *and* tell you how to improve your performance), then these improvement tips can best be described as *feedforward*. Feedforward information not only occurs in constructive feedback (whether informal or formal): you can also find useful feedforward information elsewhere in your university to aid you in future assignments (e.g. lecture notes, module descriptor, course handbook, and seminars). These sources are all around you and can focus on two types of information that can be of value to your submission: generic and subject-specific. Let's deal with generic information first. Generic information applies across departmental modules whereas subject-specific information relates to particular modules. Table 10.1 lists the more common types of generic information, including likely sources, that can help your future performance in essays and common examples of subject-specific information for essay questions.

As you can see, much feedforward information comes from documented sources (e.g. course handbook, module descriptor, departmental website, library resources, essay question). For example, the module descriptor is rich in feedforward information. Students tend to overlook the importance of the module descriptor. This is a mistake. It contains valuable information: list of topics, depth of topics to be covered, and order of topics. You can then anticipate essay questions, linking learning outcome keywords with syllabus topics and the outline teaching plan. In short, it tells you the topics that you will be assessed on, including the depth of assessment.

 A common student mistake

A common mistake by students is to pay little attention to module descriptors. They contain helpful information on the subject syllabus, reading list, as well as the number, and type, of assignments you will be assessed on. In particular, the individual learning objectives dictate the topics to be covered, including depth of study, e.g. 'The student will be able to understand the role of the Systems Analyst in the Systems Development Life Cycle'. If an essay assignment is linked to a specific topic or group of topics, then so much the better. You can then use this information to prepare for upcoming essays.

The essay question is, bizarre as it may seem, often looked at superficially by students intent on answering the question that they would like rather than the question that is asked. Chapter 5 tells you how to break down an essay question into its constituent parts using the concept of GALA, enabling a structure that ties you into answering the question asked and nothing else.

When you combine informal advice given by tutors, lecturers, and peers with documented sources, then it becomes clear that feedforward information contains much that you would do well to take on board when writing your essay. And once you start getting constructive formal feedback on your submissions, you can use that information to learn from your experiences and adjust your learning strategy and skill set accordingly.

Table 10.1 Feedforward: Generic and subject-specific information

Generic information	Main source	Subject-specific information	Main source
Generic marking scheme	Course handbook	Specific topics to be covered	Module descriptor (learning outcomes, syllabus, teaching plan); essay question
Referencing guidelines	Course handbook; departmental website; library	Depth of answer sought	Module descriptor (learning outcomes: keywords, e.g. outline, describe, analyse); tutorials/seminars; keywords used in essay question
Submission guidelines	Course handbook; assignment	Exploration and interpretation of topics	Lectures; tutorials/seminars; peers; recommended reading; library resources
Academic writing	Academic/Student Services; recommended reading; conference proceedings; journals; library resources; past submissions; tutor; peers	Assignment task	Essay question; tutors; lecturers; peers

Responding to formal feedback

Now that you understand the purpose of formal feedback, as well as the standard that formal feedback ought to meet to be of use to you and the importance of exploiting feedforward information, it is equally important that you know what to do when you receive your formal feedback.

As mentioned earlier, feedback is a learning process and ought to be viewed in that light. You are trying to improve with each new essay submission and you can only do that if you take on board any constructive advice given.

So, what should you do when you get your feedback? For the purpose of discussion, let's assume that it's formal written feedback containing your mark (e.g. 52 per cent) with comments on your essay appearing in a standard departmental feedback form. In the first instance, you need to understand what your mark means. Most departments have a generic marking scheme that explains what the different grades mean, usually divided into bands such as 70+, 60+, 50+, 40+, 30+, indicating Excellent, Very Good, Good, Pass, and Fail, respectively. Within each band, details are provided describing what you need to do to get 70+, 60+, 50+, etc.

Indeed, before you attempt your essay, you should understand what these bands, where they exist, mean; as you are writing your essay, you should be constantly checking that you meet the criteria for the band, or grade, you want to achieve; and when you get your mark back, the generic marking scheme ought to be your first port of call. For example, if the explanatory marking scheme for 70+ refers to the need to show 'in-depth analysis', then it makes sense for you to find out what counts as 'in-depth analysis'. Tutor feedback forms often include the generic marking scheme to allow students to correlate their marks against stated criteria. The outline structure of a typical tutor feedback form appears in Appendix E and is shown in Figure 10.2 for convenience.

After you have a good understanding of what your mark means, you should turn your attention to marker comments. If the marker is following criteria outlined in the 5 Cs – that is, feedback should be Clear, Concise, Consistent, Convenient, and Constructive – then the comments ought to explain in simple language why you got the mark you did. If the marker is being really helpful, then he/she will break down the feedback in terms of your strengths and weaknesses. Your strengths are areas you want to replicate in future essays; your weaknesses are areas you want to remedy.

Under a suitable heading (e.g. 'Recommendations for Improvement' or 'Learning Points'), an informative feedback sheet will also point out what you have to do to improve for next time. Even if that is not the case, it is easy to work out from the marker comments what you need to do to better your mark. For example, let's suppose that you get a mark of 52 per cent and you read the following comments about your work:

| MARKER COMMENTS

- Solid start, clearly indicating topics to be covered with confident assertion of student's stance.
- Key terms not defined (e.g. Impressionism).

Figure 10.2 Typical tutor feedback form (outline structure)

FEEDBACK SHEET	
STUDENT NUMBER:	**MARK (/100):**
ASSIGNMENT NUMBER:	

WHAT YOUR GRADE MEANS

70+:	Distinction.	Categorised by in-depth analysis ...
60+:	Very good.	A balanced essay covering most aspects ...
50+:	Good.	A competent answer that ...
40+:	Basic pass.	Limited in a number of key areas ...
<40:	Fail.	This fails to address ...

MARKER COMMENTS

RECOMMENDATIONS FOR IMPROVEMENT

Tutor signature: **Date:**

- Weighted too much towards Van Gogh's personal life and not enough on the artists and paintings that influenced his work.
- Too descriptive in nature, particularly with reference to influences.
- Good use of photographs and quotations.
- References – laudable effort to reference properly but too dependent on web sources.
- Strong conclusion, succinctly summarising key issues.

As you can see, generic issues have been highlighted (e.g. referencing) as well as module-specific issues (e.g. artists that influenced Van Gogh). This is normal practice. The comments are constructive because they offer praise where possible and suggest weaknesses that require attention. Although the marker does not structure the feedback under the convenient headings 'Strengths', 'Weaknesses', and 'Things to Do for Next Submission', nevertheless we can take the marker's comments and reallocate them verbatim under 'Strengths', 'Weaknesses', etc. as appropriate, and then deduce from the identified weaknesses what needs to be done to improve for the next submission. So, applying this approach to the marker comments:

STRENGTHS

- Solid start, clearly indicating topics to be covered with confident assertion of student's stance.
- Good use of photographs and quotations.
- References – laudable effort to reference properly.
- Strong conclusion, succinctly summarising key issues.

WEAKNESSES

- Key terms not defined (e.g. Impressionism).
- Weighted too much towards Van Gogh's personal life and not enough on the artists and paintings that influenced his work.
- Too descriptive in nature, particularly with reference to influences.
- References – too dependent on web sources.

FOR NEXT SUBMISSION

- Define key terms.
- Make sure time spent on topics reflects essay question.
- More analysis, less description.
- References: more books and scholarly articles.

You could put this information into a form of your own creation, as a record of your interpretation of your formal feedback. A suitable form is shown in Table 10.2 (a blank version appears in Appendix E for reference).

Doing this allows you to focus on what you did well, what you didn't do so well and, therefore, what you ought to do to improve your mark. Keep a record of your formal feedback, and your interpretation of that feedback, in a feedback

Table 10.2 Example student notes on formal tutor feedback

NOTES ON FORMAL TUTOR FEEDBACK
ESSAY QUESTION: Critically evaluate the influence of other artists and paintings on Van Gogh's style of art.

Grade/Mark: 52%

Date: 14 November 2018

Strengths	Weaknesses	For next submission . . .
• Solid start, clearly indicating topics to be covered with confident assertion of student's stance. • Good use of photographs and quotations. • References – laudable effort to reference properly. • Strong conclusion, succinctly summarising key issues.	• Key terms not defined (e.g. Impressionism). • Weighted too much towards Van Gogh's personal life and not enough on the artists and paintings that influenced his work. • Too descriptive in nature, particularly with reference to influences. • References – too dependent on web sources.	• Remember to define key terms. • Make sure time spent on topics reflects essay question. • More analysis, less description. • More books and scholarly articles.

folder. In effect, for each essay you will have two feedback forms: the formal feedback form from your tutor and one that you will create yourself to highlight your strengths, weaknesses, and what you have to do to improve for next submission. As your formal and personal feedback forms build up, you can track your progress (including common strengths and weaknesses).

The value of creating your own interpretation of formal tutor feedback cannot be emphasised enough. Too often tutors make the same comments to the same students who then repeat the same mistakes ad infinitum. One way to break the chain in this circle of failure is to ensure that you understand what your tutor is telling you, and the only way you can do that is if you can interpret his/her commentary. That is why a simple sheet on 'Notes on Formal Tutor Feedback', highlighting your strengths, weaknesses, and things to do for next submission could prove invaluable. It is the combined effort of tutor feedback and your translation of tutor feedback into useful headings that will influence your subsequent learning and allow corrective action to be applied and transferred into future contexts, as summarised in Figure 10.3.

After receiving your formal feedback and recording your own notes, it is recommended that you arrange a meeting with your tutor. Take your formal tutor

Figure 10.3 Breaking the feedback cycle of failure

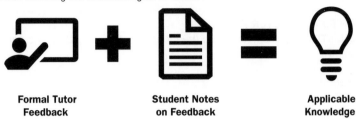

| Formal Tutor
Feedback | Student Notes
on Feedback | Applicable
Knowledge |

Figure 10.4 Email template to request feedback meeting

To:

Cc/Bcc, From:

Subject: Request for Feedback Meeting

Dear x,

Student Name: xxxx xxxxxx

Module name/number: xxxxxx

Thank you for the formal feedback for my essay (assignment number x, if more than one assignment) in part fulfilment of the module above, for which I received the mark of x. I would like to take the opportunity to discuss my essay, and learn from my submission, in particular to clarify what I did well, what I didn't do so well, and what I ought to do to improve.

If it helps here are the times when I do not have classes:

Mon:

Tues:

Wed:

Thurs:

Fri:

I look forward to hearing from you and thank you in anticipation.

Kind regards,

Xxxx Xxxxxx

feedback along with your own 'Notes on Formal Tutor Feedback' into the meeting. Creating your own feedback notes shows your tutor that you are keen to understand and learn from tutor feedback. Discuss your interpretations with your tutor. If your interpretation is wrong, then you can correct it. It is understandable that you want to remove any perceived deficiencies in your work but it is equally important that you do not forget to repeat your strengths! Figure 10.4 shows an email template that you can use to arrange a meeting with your tutor.

A final point on feedback. If you get a mark that disappoints you, then try to take it on the chin, learn from the experience, and do better next time. You can ask your tutor to justify your mark but don't expect your tutor to change it. Your tutor is the one with the subject knowledge and experience of marking. Haranguing your tutor for a better mark is a fruitless task, not to mention unseemly: academic judgement is normally not open to challenge in universities. In fact, many universities make this very point in their complaints procedure.

On the other hand, if you feel that you have been treated unfairly or suffered as a result of teaching or resource deficiencies or because a tutor did not adhere to university procedures (e.g. not following university feedback protocol), then you may have recourse to the university complaints procedure. Even then, the university may thank you for your feedback and take steps to improve their teaching (or resources or adherence to protocol) but decide that the academic judgement of your marker was sound and so leave your mark unchanged. Furthermore, if most students passed and some obtained merit – reflecting average university scores – then that may diminish any argument that teaching (or resource issues or failure to follow university protocol) impacted adversely on your mark.

If you are genuinely interested in improving teaching (or resources, etc.), then raise these issues with your student representative during the semester (your student representative should make themselves known to you but their contact details can normally be found on a department's web page, the university's Virtual Learning Environment, or by contacting the Students' Associations or the departmental secretary for your course). Universities are keen on meeting students' needs and do take on board any suggestions/concerns raised by student representatives. Don't use your student representative as a first port of call to complain about a tutor – you should make every effort to resolve matters at an informal level, starting with your tutor in the first instance. Misunderstandings do happen. For example, a tutor who is explaining to you where you are going wrong is not 'getting at you'. On the contrary, it is an attempt to make you a better student.

If you are experiencing health problems or domestic issues, then you need to report these as early as possible with Student Services (they are very good at liaising with departments and getting the support you need) and/or your tutor. In such circumstances, an extension or alternative means of assessment may be possible. Reporting matters that you feel impacted adversely on your submission, and therefore your mark, is much more difficult to deal with after you have received your mark.

Tutors are there to help you and will go that extra mile to help you. Nothing pleases them more than to see their students get good marks; but, they are also guardians of academic standards. If you have a problem, academic or otherwise, then go and discuss it with them and/or Student Services as early as possible. That gives everyone time to try and manage the situation and to work out a way forward.

Above all, learn from tutor feedback with a view to improving with each new submission. In that way, you will enhance your understanding of the word 'student'.

Summary of key points

- *Formal* feedback is normally associated with tutor-graded assessments.
- *Informal* feedback occurs in everyday situations.
- Feedback can be given in writing or verbally and can come from a variety of sources, including tutors, peers, and self-assessment.
- Feedforward is a concept that is based on taking information from both documented sources and advice, hints, etc. from everyday situations, to improve future performance. Information from formal feedback (i.e. assessed performance) will also be used to feedforward into future submissions.
- Formal feedback should meet the 5 Cs. That is, it should be Clear, Concise, Consistent, Convenient, and Constructive.
- Based on your formal feedback, create your own summary form highlighting your strengths, weaknesses, and things to do to improve future submissions.
- Keep a record of your formal feedback, and your interpretation of that feedback, in a feedback folder.
- Make an appointment to speak to your tutor to clarify that your interpretation of your strengths, etc. is correct.
- Formal feedback is best viewed as a learning opportunity and ought to be approached in that light to achieve optimum benefit.
- If you have an issue that impacts adversely on your studies, then seek help immediately – don't leave it until after you have received an unfavourable grade.

11 # Summary essay template of good practice

Essay template

Use the summary essay template in Figure 11.1 and the notes that follow on good practice as a quick reference guide.

Figure 11.1 Summary essay template

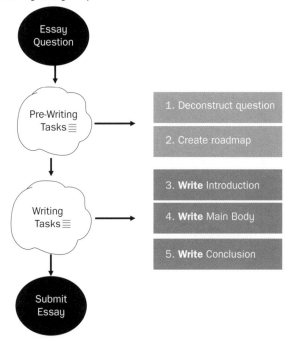

Notes on essay template and good practice

Step 1: Deconstruct question

Using Table 11.1, apply GALA to identify the **G**eneral essay topic (e.g. art), any **A**spect of that topic that you have been asked to focus on (e.g. Impressionism), any **L**imiting words (e.g. three paintings), and the **A**ction word(s) used (e.g. assess) including definition(s), then rewrite the essay question, substituting any action words with their dictionary definitions.

Table 11.1 Gala template

Essay Question:	
	Question Deconstruction
General topic area:	
Aspect of general topic to be addressed:	
Limiting word(s):	
Action word(s):	

Step 2: Create a roadmap

Paying particular attention to the meaning of the action word(s) used, fit the results of GALA into the generic essay template (Introduction – Background – Main Body – Conclusion – References) to give a clear roadmap of the ground that you intend to cover in your essay:

- Introduction
- Background: . . .
- Topic 1
- Topic 2
- . . .
- . . .
- Conclusion
- References

Step 3: Write the Introduction

Keep your Introduction to one short paragraph. A good Introduction can contain up to four elements:

1 A contextual comment (one sentence, two at most).
2 What you are going to write about (one sentence, two at most).

3 Your stance/position (one sentence).
4 A reference or two.[1,2]

Step 4: Write Main Body

The Main Body is in two parts: a small Background section followed by the Main Body proper. The Background section is where you set the scene. Typically, the Background section is where you will describe whatever it is you intend analysing/evaluating, etc. in the Main Body proper. Any terms that require to be defined would also form part of your Background section. The Main Body proper is where you answer the essay question.[3-5]

Step 5: Write the Conclusion

Keep your Conclusion to one paragraph, two at most. Do not introduce any new arguments or evidence in your Conclusion. A good Conclusion contains a number of activities:

1 A restatement of your stance.
2 A summary of your main points.
3 Either recommendations on the way forward, 'food for thought', or both.[6]

Give credit where credit is due!

Plagiarism is where you take credit for someone else's work, in whole or part, and claim it as your own. The antidote to plagiarism is referencing. You reference a source in two places in your essay: in-text (i.e. in the body of your essay) and in a reference list at the end of your essay – this is handily titled 'References'! For every source that you cite in-text, you need a corresponding entry – showing full published details – in the References section. Your references ought to be:

1 reasonably recent;
2 relevant;
3 reliable;
4 of sufficient quantity;
5 formatted in line with academic standards.

The language that you use

Some pointers:

- Paragraphs are the building blocks of university essays. Keep your paragraphs focused and coherent and start each with a topical sentence.
- Punctuation is the glue that holds sentences together. Learn how to apply this glue.

- There are many differences in spelling between British English and American English. Be consistent.
- Sometimes numbers have to be spelled out (e.g. double-digit numbers and above). Pick a system for writing numbers and stick to it.
- There are verbs that you can use to show a neutral position, a favoured position, or when casting doubt. Pick the one that reflects what you want to write.
- Learn the tricks of writing, from alliteration, to useful Latin terms, to exploiting metaphors and similes, to the occasional short paragraph. And even consider shorter sentences.
- Understand the words that students often conflate, and you won't get confused.

Writing a university essay is more craft than art.

Hopefully, this book has given you the particular skills and knowledge to succeed with your university essay.

Notes

1 The language that you use: The formal stuff

1 The hyphen is not used to indicate a range of numbers. A different sign is used – the en sign.
2 There is an exception here in British English, where 'judgment' is preferred in the case of legal or judicial proceedings.
3 Journalists always use 'Celsius', not 'Centigrade' – the old-fashioned word for Celsius – or 'Fahrenheit': 12°C, 64°C, 80°C, etc.
4 There is no need to include the degree symbol, e.g. 12C rather than 12°C.
5 From 1977–80 is redundant. Correct version: from 1977 to 1980.
6 Omit date abbreviations for first, second, third, etc. (e.g. use 1, 2, and 3 instead of 1st, 2nd and 3rd).

2 The language that you use: The fancy stuff

1 This section was influenced by William Safire's little gem of a book, *How not to write*. Full publication details: Safire, W. (1999) *How not to write: The essential misrules of grammar*. New York: The Cobbett Corporation.
2 This section was influenced by Simon Heffer's excellent book, *Strictly English*. Specifically, pp. 136–165. Full publication details: Heffer, S. (2011) *Strictly English: The correct way to write*. London: Windmill Books.
3 Note for the geeks. *Unconscious* can mean thoughts and feelings that lie hidden below our conscious. In fact, it is a specialist term used by psychologists and psychiatrists to mean just that, but it tends to relate to repressed memories (things we'd like to forget). These very same specialists recognise that there is also the *subconscious*, thoughts that lie between the conscious and the unconscious. We can access subconscious thoughts if we want to, e.g. when we go home we do not consciously think about how to get home ('I need to turn right here, pass the shops, then go up the hill') – it is a subconscious act. Most people (i.e. non-specialists) use the word 'unconscious' when they mean subconscious (e.g. it is unlikely that knowing the way to walk home without thinking is a repressed memory, or buying goods is a repressed memory, or voting a certain way is a repressed memory, etc.). The problem is complicated further by the fact that specialists themselves disagree about the definitions of the unconscious/subconscious mind, and the level of interplay between the two. Added to the mix is that there is also a medical term for *unconscious*, meaning 'knocked out'.

4 One has a sneaking suspicion that this debate is more about a desire to return to an age where 'proper' English, or lack thereof, helped differentiate the daintily perfumed from the great unwashed, i.e. it is more a signifier of class than it is about improving communication.

3 Give credit where credit is due

1 Given the core nature of this topic in academia, from undergraduate to postgraduate study, much of this chapter is replicated from the following book, by the same author: Biggam, J. (2018) *Succeeding with your master's dissertation: A step-by-step handbook*. 4th edn. London: Open University Press.

2 For conference papers you include what information you have. If it is published, give the publishing details; if it is viewed online, give the URL details; if it is not available online, then give the conference details.

3 'Proceedings of' means from a collection of conference papers.

4 Interpret 'pp.' to mean plural pages. So. pp. 5–15 means pages 5 to 15 inclusive.

4 The hierarchy of essay questions

1 This hierarchy equally applies to a university dissertation. See Biggam, J. *Succeeding with your master's dissertation: A step-by-step handbook*. 4th edition. London: Open University Press.

5 Step 1: Deconstruct the essay question using GALA

1 In this example, the essay question happens to give part of the definition of the action word. *Describe* means to give in detail the main characteristics of something. Also, 'With reference to' is both an action word and a limiting term.

2 Very often the action word *evaluate* is preceded by the action word *critically* to emphasise that a rigorous balanced debate is expected in your essay, as in *Critically evaluate the usefulness of social media as a marketing tool*. In effect, there is no real difference between *evaluate* and *critically evaluate* – the latter is purely a technique for emphasis.

6 Step 2: Create a roadmap

1 In this example, the essay question happens to give part of the definition of the action word. *Describe* means to give in detail the main characteristics of

something. That is why, after inserting the definition of the action word *describe*, there is not much difference between the original question and the reinterpretation of the essay question.

8 Step 4: Write the Main Body

1 Conclusions are discussed in Chapter 9.

9 Step 5: Conclude your essay

1 There are exceptions to this rule; not all essays are of the type that involve making recommendations. For example, purely descriptive essays are an exception. Hence, the (sometimes) optional nature of the third activity.

11 Summary essay template of good practice

1 Elements (2) and (3) are interchangeable in terms of when they occur in your Introduction.
2 If your essay is of the type that does not require a position on your part (e.g. it is descriptive in nature), then element (3) is omitted.
3 Avoid *student drift* by erecting hierarchical signposts (i.e. by creating sub-headings under your main essay headings). These subheadings, as well as your main headings, can be removed prior to submission of your essay.
4 Avoid the trap of spending too much time *describing* things (unless the essay question specifically asks you to do that). Most university essays demand evidence of a higher-level skill, such as the ability to assess or analyse or evaluate (i.e. evidence of critical commentary).
5 As we saw in Chapter 8, the process for providing critical commentary is captured in the formula:

cc = describe something + [make a point about that something + support with evidence]

6 You can use a quotation in your Conclusion but make it short, relevant, self-explanatory, follow from the preceding sentence, and the last thing that you write.

Appendix A: Useful verbs

Accepts	Acknowledges	Acquiesces	Adduces
Admits	Adopts	Advances	Advises
Advocates	Agrees	Alludes	Appears
Argues	Arrives at	Articulates	Asserts
Assumes	Attempts	Bombasts	Bores
Builds	Cajoles	Calculates	Captures
Cautions	Challenges	Clarifies	Clings
Clutches	Comments	Compares	Compiles
Complains	Concludes	Concocts	Concurs
Confirms	Confuses	Considers	Conspires
Constructs	Contemplates	Contends	Contrives
Conveys	Convinces	Cultivates	Dabbles
Debates	Debunks	Declares	Deduces
Defends	Delves	Demonstrates	Denounces
Denies	Derides	Derives	Desists
Determines	Develops	Digresses	Dilutes
Disagrees	Discloses	Discovers	Discusses
Dismisses	Dispels	Dispenses	Displays
Disputes	Dissects	Dissents	Distils
Distinguishes	Distorts	Diverges	Diverts
Dodges	Drags	Drifts	Earns
Eases	Echoes	Effaces	Effects
Effuses	Elaborates	Elucidates	Embarks
Embellishes	Embraces	Emphasises	Employs
Enables	Enchants	Endears	Endorses
Engages	Engineers	Enlightens	Enthrals
Entices	Enunciates	Epitomises	Equates
Erects	Errs	Eschews	Espouses
Establishes	Evaluates	Evangelises	Evokes
Exaggerates	Excels	Exhibits	Expands
Explains	Explores	Expresses	Expunges
Extricates	Fabricates	Faces	Fails
Falters	Favours	Fawns	Feigns
Ferments	Fiddles	Fields	Finds
Fluctuates	Forges	Forms	Formulates
Fortifies	Frees	Fulfils	Fusses
Gambles	Gathers	Gauges	Generates
Gets	Gilds	Gives	Glides
Glorifies	Grafts	Grapples	Grasps
Grates	Grinds	Gropes	Guesses

Hampers	Handles	Hankers	Has
Hatches	Hedges	Helps	Heralds
Hesitates	Highlights	Hijacks	Hikes
Hinders	Holds	Identifies	Ignores
Illuminates	Illustrates	Imagines	Imbues
Imparts	Impedes	Impels	Impinges
Implants	Implicates	Implies	Implores
Imposes	Impregnates	Impresses	Improves
Impugns	Imputes	Incites	Inclines
Includes	Inculcates	Indicates	Induces
Indulges	Infers	Infests	Inflames
Inflates	Inflicts	Influences	Informs
Infringes	Inhibits	Injects	Inquires
Insinuates	Insists	Inspects	Inspires
Instigates	Instructs	Insults	Integrates
Intends	Interferes	Interjects	Interprets
Intertwines	Interweaves	Intimates	Introduces
Intrudes	Inundates	Invalidates	Inveighs
Invents	Investigates	Invigorates	Invites
Involves	Irritates	Iterates	Joins
Jostles	Jumps	Justifies	Juxtaposes
Knows	Kowtows	Labours	Lacerates
Lags	Laments	Lampoons	Lances
Lapses	Lauds	Launches	Lays
Leads	Leans	Learns	Lectures
Lends	Lets	Likes	Limps
Lingers	Links	Lists	Litters
Livens	Loads	Lobs	Locates
Loiters	Looks	Lurches	Magnifies
Maintains	Makes	Maligns	Maltreats
Manages	Manifests	Marks	Marvels
Massages	Masters	Mauls	Means
Measures	Meddles	Mediates	Mentions
Merges	Merits	Militates	Milks
Minces	Miscalculates	Misfires	Misinforms
Misinterprets	Misjudges	Misleads	Misrepresents
Misses	Mistakes	Misunderstands	Misuses
Mitigates	Mixes	Moans	Mocks
Models	Modifies	Modulates	Motivates
Moulds	Mounts	Moves	Muddles
Mulls	Muses	Musters	Nags
Names	Narrates	Needs	Negates
Neglects	Negotiates	Niggles	Notes
Notices	Nullifies	Nurtures	Obeys
Obfuscates	Objects	Obliges	Obliterates

Obscures	Observes	Obsesses	Obstructs
Obtains	Occupies	Offends	Offers
Omits	Oozes	Operates	Opposes
Oppresses	Opts	Ordains	Organises
Oscillates	Ostracises	Outlines	Outwits
Overawes	Overcomes	Overindulges	Overlooks
Overreaches	Overreacts	Overworks	Pads
Paints	Panders	Panics	Papers
Parables	Paraphrases	Participates	Peddles
Penetrates	Pens	Peppers	Perceives
Percolates	Perfects	Performs	Permeates
Permits	Perpetrates	Perpetuates	Perseveres
Persists	Personifies	Persuades	Pervades
Perverts	Pierces	Pilfers	Pillories
Pinions	Pioneers	Placates	Places
Plans	Plods	Plucks	Plugs
Plummets	Plunders	Plunges	Poaches
Points	Pollutes	Ponders	Pontificates
Populates	Portends	Portrays	Poses
Positions	Possess	Postulates	Postures
Praises	Prances	Prattles	Preaches
Precedes	Precipitates	Predicts	Pre-empts
Prefers	Prejudices	Prepares	Prescribes
Presents	Preserves	Presses	Presumes
Pretends	Prevails	Prevaricates	Prevents
Probes	Processes	Proclaims	Procures
Prods	Produces	Professes	Proffers
Profiles	Profits	Profligates	Progresses
Proliferates	Promotes	Prompts	Pronounces
Propagates	Proposes	Propounds	Proscribes
Prostrates	Protests	Provides	Provokes
Publishes	Puffs	Pulverises	Pursues
Pushes	Puts	Qualifies	Quantifies
Quarrels	Queries	Questions	Quibbles
Quotes	Radiates	Rages	Raises
Rallies	Rambles	Rants	Rates
Rationalises	Raves	Reaches	Reacts
Realises	Reasons	Reassures	Rebels
Rebuffs	Rebukes	Rebuts	Recants
Receives	Reciprocates	Recites	Reckons
Recognises	Recommends	Reconciles	Reconsiders
Reconstructs	Records	Recreates	Rectifies
Redeems	Redresses	Reduces	Refers
Reflects	Reforms	Refrains	Refuses
Regales	Regards	Regrets	Reinforces

Reiterates	Rejects	Relapses	Relates
Relents	Relies	Relishes	Remains
Remarks	Remedies	Reminds	Removes
Renders	Repairs	Repeats	Repels
Repents	Replies	Reports	Represents
Reprimands	Reproaches	Repudiates	Repulses
Requests	Requires	Rescinds	Rescues
Researches	Resembles	Resents	Resists
Resolves	Resorts	Respects	Responds
Restricts	Retains	Retracts	Retreats
Retrieves	Reveals	Reviews	Revises
Revokes	Resolves	Ridicules	Rids
Rues	Ruminates	Sabotages	Sacrifices
Salvages	Samples	Sanctions	Satirises
Satisfies	Savages	Schemes	Scintillates
Scorns	Scrambles	Scrapes	Scrutinises
Searches	Secures	Seems	Sees
Seizes	Selects	Sends	Senses
Separates	Serves	Sets	Settles
Shapes	Shares	Shies	Shifts
Shines	Shirks	Shocks	Shoulders
Shows	Shrinks	Shrouds	Shuns
Shuts	Signals	Signifies	Simplifies
Simulates	Sinks	Sketches	Skims
Skips	Skirts	Slams	Slanders
Slants	Slays	Slights	Slings
Slips	Slots	Smears	Smothers
Snubs	Softens	Solicits	Solidifies
Solves	Sorts	Sources	Sparks
Spearheads	Speculates	Spends	Spins
Spoils	Spots	Spouts	Spreads
Squabbles	Squanders	Squares	Stands
Starts	States	Stiffens	Stimulates
Stirs	Stops	Strafes	Strains
Strays	Strengthens	Stresses	Stretches
Strives	Structures	Struts	Studies
Stumbles	Subjects	Submits	Subscribes
Substantiates	Subverts	Succeeds	Succumbs
Suffers	Suffices	Suggests	Summarises
Supplants	Supplies	Supports	Supposes
Suppresses	Surmises	Surmounts	Surpasses
Surrounds	Surveys	Suspects	Sustains
Sways	Symbolises	Sympathises	Synthesises
Tabulates	Taints	Takes	Talks
Tarnishes	Taunts	Teases	Teeters

Tempers	Tempts	Tends	Terminates
Testifies	Tests	Thanks	Theorises
Thrives	Thrusts	Tirades	Toils
Tolerates	Touches	Traces	Tracks
Transcends	Transforms	Transgresses	Transmits
Traverses	Treats	Tricks	Tries
Trifles	Triumphs	Trivialises	Trumpets
Trumps	Tweaks	Typifies	Unburdens
Undercuts	Underestimates	Undergoes	Underlines
Undermines	Underrates	Understands	Understates
Undertakes	Undervalues	Unearths	Unfolds
Unifies	Unites	Unloads	Unlocks
Unravels	Untangles	Unties	Unveils
Unwinds	Upholds	Upsets	Urges
Uses	Utilises	Validates	Values
Vents	Ventures	Verges	Views
Vilifies	Vindicates	Violates	Vituperates
Vocalises	Voices	Volunteers	Wades
Waffles	Wallows	Wanders	Wants
Warms	Warrants	Wastes	Wavers
Waxes	Weaves	Welcomes	Wheedles
Whines	Whittles	Wills	Winds
Wishes	Withdraws	Withers	Withstands
Witnesses	Wobbles	Wonders	Works
Wrenches	Wrestles	Wriggles	Wrings
Writes	Yanks	Yearns	Yields
Zaps	Zings	Zips	

Appendix B: Harvard referencing templates (with examples)

The following reference templates are based on the style of Harvard referencing advocated by Pears and Shields (2019) in their popular book *Cite Them Right*.

Artwork

Artwork in gallery

Artist (year) *Title* [Medium]. Gallery name, City.

Rembrandt, van R. (1642) *Night watch* [Oil on canvas]. Rijkmuseum, Amsterdam.

If viewed online:

Artist (year) *Title* [Medium]. Available at: URL (Accessed: date).

Rembrandt, van R. (1642) *Night watch* [Oil on canvas]. Available at: https://www.rijksmuseum.nl/en/search/objects?q=Rembrandt+&p=1&ps=12&st=OBJECTS&ii=2#/SK-C-5,2 (Accessed: 10 April 2007).

Temporary exhibition

Title of exhibition (year) [Exhibition]. Place exhibited. Date(s) of exhibition.

NoNoseKnows (2015) [Exhibition]. Glasgow International 2016, Tramway Gallery. 8–25 April 2016.

If viewed online:

Title of exhibition (year) [Exhibition]. Available at: URL (Accessed: date).

A world view: John Latham (2017) [Exhibition]. Available at: http://www.serpentinegalleries.org/exhibitions-events/world-view-john-latham (Accessed 19 March 2017).

Artwork in public space

Artist (year) *Title* [Medium]. Location, City.

Niki de Saint Phalle (1996) *Tympanum* [Mirror mosaic]. Glasgow Gallery of Modern Art, Scotland.

Exhibition catalogue

Author (year) *Title of exhibition*. Place of exhibition, date(s) of exhibition [Exhibition catalogue].

Humphrey, P. (2012) *The Essence of Beauty: 500 Years of Italian Art*. Exhibition held in Kelvingrove Art Gallery and Museum, Glasgow, 6 April–12 August 2012 [Exhibition catalogue].

Article found on the internet

Author's surname, initials (year) 'Title of article'. Available at: URL (Accessed: date).

Haseman, B. (2006) 'A manifesto for performative research'. Available at: http://eprints.qut.edu.au/3999/1/3999_1.pdf (Accessed: 12 January 2017)

Book

Author's surname, initials (year) *Title of book*. Edition if not first. Place of publication: Publisher.

Neville, C. (2016) *The complete guide to referencing and avoiding plagiarism*. 3rd edn. London: Open University Press.

Chapter in a book:

Author's surname, initials (year) 'Title of chapter', in Editor name(s) (eds) *Title of book*. Place of publication: Publisher, page(s).

Elsky, M. (1982) 'Words, things, and names: Jonson's poetry and philosophical grammar', in Summers, C. J. and Pebworth, T. L. (eds) *Classic and cavalier: essays on Jonson and the sons of Ben*. Pittsburgh, PA: University of Pittsburgh Press, pp. 31–44.

E-book

Author's surname, initials (year) *Title of book*. Edition if not first. Available at: URL (Accessed: date).

Taylor, M. and Mayled, J. (2009) *OCR Philosophy of Religion*. Available at: https://www.amazon.co.uk/OCR-Philosophy-Religion-AS-A2/dp/0415468248 (Downloaded: 18 March 2017).

Cinema film

Title of film (Year) Directed by director name [Film]. Place of distribution: distributor.

> *King: Skull Island* (2017) Directed by Jordan Vogt-Roberts [Film]. California: Warner Bros.

Classical music

Musical score

Composer (Year) *Title*. Additional information. Place of publication: publisher.

> Chopin, F. (2009) *Mazarkus*. Edited by Carl Mikuli. New York: Dover Publications.

If viewed online:

Composer (Year) *Title*. Additional information. Available at: URL (Accessed: date).

> Kratz, T. (2016) *Joy*. For piano. Available at: https://www.kratz/joy (Accessed: 14 May 2017).

Live performance

Composer (Year performed) *Title*. Performed by orchestra name conducted by conductor name [Place performed. Date seen].

> Korngold, E. W. (2017) *Symphony in F sharp*. Performed by the Scottish Symphony Orchestra conducted by John Wilson [City Halls, Glasgow. 16 March 2017].

Company report

Author or Company Name (Year) *Title*. Place of publication: publisher.

> Tesco (2016) *Strategic report*. London: Addison Group.

If viewed online:

Author/Company (Year) *Title*. Available at: URL (Accessed: date).

> Tesco (2016) *Strategic report*. Available at: https://www.tescoplc.com/ media/264194/annual-report-2016.pdf (Accessed: 10 October 2017).

Conference paper

Author's surname, initials (year) 'Title of paper', *Title of conference*, location, dates of conference. Place of publication: publisher, page(s).

Bloom, J. (2017) 'Picasso turns blue', *Straight from the artist's mouth*, Art Institute, Falkirk, 2–3 March 2015. London: Artbooks, pp. 36–40.

If viewed online:

Author's surname, initials (year) 'Title of paper', *Title of conference*, location, dates of conference, page(s) if available. Available at: URL (Accessed: date).

Conole, G., Oliver, M., Isroff, K. and Ravenscroft, A. (2004) 'Addressing methodological issues in e-learning research', *Proceedings of the Networked Learning Conference*, Lancaster University, UK, 5–7 April. Available at: www.sef.ac.uk/nlc/Proceedings/Symposa4.htm (Accessed: 2 October 2004).

Or (using *et al.*):

Conole, G. *et al.* (2004) 'Addressing methodological issues in e-learning research', *Proceedings of the Networked Learning Conference*, Lancaster University, UK, 5–7 April. Available at: www.sef.ac.uk/nlc/Proceedings/ Symposa4.htm (Accessed: 2 October 2004).

Government publication

Author's surname, initials (year) *Title of publication*, Place of publication: Publisher.

Goulding, A. and Cavanagh, B. (2013) *Charges reported under the Offensive Behaviour at Football and Threatening Communications (Scotland) Act in 2012–2013*, Edinburgh: Scottish Government Social Research.

If viewed online:

Author's surname, initials (year) *Title of publication*, Place of publication: Publisher. Available at: URL (Accessed: date).

Sosenko, F., Livingstone, N. and Fitzpatrick, S. (2013) *Overview of food aid provision in Scotland*, Edinburgh: Scottish Government Social Research. Available at: http://www.gov.scot/Resource/0044/00440458.pdf (Accessed: 23 July 2016).

If author unknown, but government department known:

Department name (year) *Title of publication*, Place of publication: Publisher.

Justice Analytical Services (2013) *An Examination of the evidence of sectarianism in Scotland*, Edinburgh: Scottish Government Social Research.

If viewed online:

Department name (year) *Title of publication*, Place of publication: Publisher. Available at: URL (Accessed: date).

Animal Health and Welfare Division (2013) *Promoting responsible dog ownership in Scotland: microchipping and other measures*, Edinburgh: APS Group Scotland. Available at: http://www.gov.scot/Resource/0044/00441549.pdf (Accessed: 14 March 2014).

Journal article

Author's surname, initials (year) 'Title of article', *Name of Journal*, volume number (issue number), page(s).

Burns, E. (1994) 'Information assets, technology and organisation', *Management Science*, 40(12), pp. 645–662.

If viewed online:

Author's surname, initials (year) 'Title of article', *Name of Journal*, volume number (issue number), page(s) if available. Available at: URL (Accessed: date).

Gwatipeda, J. and Barbier, E. B. (2013) 'Environmental regulation of a global pollution externality in a bilateral trade environment: the case of global warming, China and the US', *Economics*, 2013 (60), pp. 1–43. Available at: http://www.economics-ejournal.org/economics/discussionpapers/2013-60 (Accessed: 18 August 2014).

Module material

Tutor name (Year) 'Title'. *Module number: module title*. Available at: URL (Accessed: date).

Newspaper article

Author's surname, initials (year) 'Title of article', *Name of Newspaper*, day and month of publication, page(s).

Riddell, P. and Webster, P. (2006) 'Support for Labour at lowest level since 1992', *The Times*, 9 May, p. 2.

Where the author is not known, then use the name of the newspaper instead:

Name of newspaper (year) 'Title of article', day and month of publication, page(s).

The Indian Agra News (2007) 'Carbon footprints and economic globalisation', 18 April, p. 4.

If viewed online:

Author's surname, initials (year) 'Title of article', *Name of Newspaper*, day and month of publication. Available at: URL (Accessed: date).

McArdle, H. (2013) 'Officials say new Forth bridge on schedule', *The Herald*, 30 December. Available at: http://www.heraldscotland.com/news/13138238.Officials_say_new_Forth_bridge_on_schedule/ (Accessed: 30 December 2013).

Where the author is not known, then use the name of the newspaper instead:

Name of newspaper (year) 'Title of article', day and month of publication. Available at: URL (Accessed: date).

The Herald (2013) 'Officials say new Forth bridge on schedule', 30 December. Available at: http://www.heraldscotland.com/news/13138238.Officials_say_new_Forth_bridge_on_schedule/(Accessed: 30 December 2013).

Photograph

Photographer (Year) *Title* [Photograph]. Place of publication: publisher.

Eisenstaedt, A. (1945) *The kiss* [Photograph]. New York City: Life.

If viewed online:

Photographer (Year) *Title* [Photograph]. Available at: URL (Accessed: date).

Eisenstaedt, A. (1945) *The Kiss* [Photograph]. Available at: http://100photos.time.com/photos/kiss-v-j-day-times-square-alfred-eisenstaedt (Accessed: 27 May 2017).

Play

Book format

Playwright's surname, initials (year) *Title of play*. Editor. Place of publication: Publisher.

Beckett, S. (2006) *Waiting for Godot*. Edited by Knowlson, J. London: Faber and Faber.

Live performance

Title of play by playwright (Year performed) Directed by director name [Place performed. Date seen].

The Steamie by Tony Roper (2013) Directed by Tony Roper [Eastwood Park Theatre, Scotland. 23 October 2013].

Radio programme

Title of radio programme (Year) Station, date.

Bob Harris Sunday (2017) BBC Radio 2, 19 March 2017.

Social media

Blog

Author (Year site posted) 'Title of article', *Title of site*, date posted. Available at: URL (Accessed: date).

Snowdon, K. (2012) 'Rescuing lions — an exclusive interview with Captured in Africa', *Kate on conservation*, 28 April 2016. Available at: https://kateconservation.wordpress.com/2016/04/28/rescuing-lions-an-exclusive-interview-with-captured-in-africa/ (Accessed: 27 April 2017).

Facebook

Title (Year page posted) [Facebook] date posted. Available at: URL (Accessed: date).

University of Liverpool (2017) [Facebook] 20 March. Available at: https://www.facebook.com/UniversityofLiverpool/ (Accessed: 22 March 2017).

Twitter

Author (Year of tweet) [Twitter] date posted. Available at: URL (Accessed: date).

Obama, B. (2017) [Twitter] 8 March. Available at: https://mobile.twitter.com/BarackObama?ref_src=twsrc%5Egoogle%7Ctwcamp%5Eserp%7Ctwgr%5Eauthor (Accessed: 22 March 2017).

YouTube

Name of poster (Year video posted) *Title of video*. Available at: URL (Accessed: date).

Newspoliticsinfo (2015) *Martin Luther King's last speech 'I've been to the mountain top'*. Available at: https://m.youtube.com/watch?v=Oeh-ry1JC9Rk (Accessed: 14 January 2016).

Software (computer program, mobile app, video game, etc.)

Author (year of release) *Title* (Version) [Format, e.g. Computer program, Mobile app, Video game, Xbox 360]. Distributor: Place of distribution.

If e-software:

Author/publisher (year of release) *Title* (Version) [Format, e.g. Computer program, Mobile app, Video game, Xbox 360]. Available at: URL (Downloaded: date).

AGT Technologies (2017) *AVG anti-virus* (free) [Mobile app]. Available at: http://www.avg.com/gb-en/antivirus-for-android (Downloaded: 14 March 2017.

Television

Title (Year broadcast) Channel, date.

Dr Who (2014) BBC One, 15 April 2014.

Specific episode of a series:

'Episode title' (Year) *Series title*, Series number, episode number. Channel, date.

'The Zygon Inversion' (2015) *Dr Who*, series 9, episode 8, BBC One, 13 November 2015.

Theses and dissertations

Author's name, initials (year) *Title of thesis/dissertation*. Level of award. Institution.

Aitken, R. (2008) *Exploring the role of laughter in the workplace.* PhD thesis. Inverclyde University.

If viewed online:

Author's name, initials (year) *Title of thesis/dissertation.* Level of award. Institution. Available at: URL (Accessed: date).

Website

Author's name, initials (year) *Title of web page.* Available at: URL (Accessed: date).

Brender, A. (2004) *Speakers promote distance education to audiences in Asia.* Available at: www.chronicle.com (Accessed: 12 November 2015).

If no author, then use website name or organisation name.

Appendix C: Action words in essay questions

Action word(s)	Meaning
Account for	Give an explanation or reason for something.
Analyse	Examine in detail by breaking a subject down into its constituent parts, identifying and explaining the main characteristics of these parts and the nature of the relationship between the parts, including implications.
Annotate	Add explanatory notes to a diagram or document.
Apply	Show through the use of relevant examples.
Argue against	Attack a position, justifying points made.
Argue for	Defend a position, justifying points made.
Assess	Estimate the worth/value of something by weighing up the advantages and disadvantages, strengths and weaknesses, or arguments for and against.
Calculate	Arrive at a numerical value or to establish through reason an estimate.
Choose	Select an option.
Clarify	Make clear, shed light on.
Classify	Label or group things based on distinguishing characteristics.
Comment on	Express an opinion.
Compare	Show similarities and/or differences where they exist.
Compare and contrast	Show similarities and differences. (*Compare* alone has the same meaning but *compare and contrast* adds emphasis to both tasks.)
Consider	Think about and give your reasoned viewpoint(s), arriving at an argued position.
Contrast	Show differences
Critically . . .	An in-depth, informed, and balanced discussion on the merits or otherwise of something.
Criticise	Find fault with, justifying your criticisms.
Critique	(See *Critically . . . .*)

Appendix C   Continued

Action word(s)	Meaning
Deduce	Arrive at a logical conclusion from a reasoned argument.
Defend	Support a position, giving reasons.
Define	Give the meaning of, interpret, clarify.
Demonstrate	Convince using clear explanations and examples.
Describe	Capture the main features of something or relate an event in detail.
Determine	Establish something based on a clear and justified narrative.
Develop	Take something – an idea, an issue – as a basis and expand it, providing more detail.
Diagrammatically	Use a form of diagram (e.g. graph, chart or spider diagram), i.e. any appropriate drawing, to illustrate something.
Differentiate	Show the differences.
Discuss	To debate an issue in the round, i.e. from different perspectives, including pros and cons, for and against, advantages and disadvantages, and in doing so come to a balanced conclusion.
Distinguish	To separate, explaining perceived differences.
Elaborate	(See *Develop*.)
Enumerate	Create a numbered or bullet-point list of concisely constructed points.
Evaluate	Judge the worth – value – of something by appraising its benefits and limitations, using reliable sources as evidence.
Examine	To put something under a microscope (metaphorically speaking) and so look at it in great detail with a very analytical eye, providing an in-depth narrative of what you have found.
Expand	(See *Develop*.)
Explain	Bring clarity to a topic by defining and interpreting what something means and/or provide detailed reasons for its occurrence (how and why) and/or implications.
Explore	Investigate a topic in detail, casting an inquisitive and probing eye, discussing options and implications. *Explore* questions are normally associated with scenarios, real or imagined.
Extrapolate	To take someone else's work/findings and extend further in application so as to arrive at a wider conclusion.

(continued)

Appendix C Continued

Action word(s)	Meaning
How	Explain the causes of, or reasons for, something.
How far	Explain the extent to which something has impacted (or might or should impact) on something else.
Identify	Pinpoint the main cause(s)/feature(s) of, or option(s)/solution(s) for, something.
Illustrate	Make clear through the use of examples and/or diagrams.
Infer	Show the logical implications of something.
Interpolate	Estimate from available evidence.
Interpret	Explain the meaning of something.
Justify	Provide reasons in support of something.
List	Create a numbered or bullet-point list of concisely constructed points.
Outline	Give a summary/sketch of main points/general features only.
Propose	Put forward a plan/solution.
Prove	Demonstrate the truth of a claim through rigorous argument using supporting evidence.
Relate	(1) Recount or narrate an event; or (2) show how two or more things are connected.
Review	Go over something with a critical eye, explaining its merits or otherwise, justifying points made.
Select	Pick an option.
Show (how)	Convince using clear explanations and examples.
State	Clearly express a point, or points, in a succinct manner, using examples and rationale where appropriate.
Summarise	Give a brief account, capturing the main points.
To what extent	Judge how far something applies or is relevant.
Trace	Sketch the path of some event from its origins (unless alternative date is supplied).
Use	Apply a methodology, a tool, a theory, etc. to perform a task. Similar to *With reference to*.
Use a diagram	(See *Diagrammatically*.)

Appendix C Continued

Action word(s)	Meaning
Verify	Establish the truth or correctness of something through in-depth examination, using clear explanations and examples.
What	Identify and explain something.
When	Identify time frames, or specific triggers for an event.
Where	Identify locations, justifying your answer.
Which	Select an option, justifying your answer.
Why	Provide an explanation of, or explanations for, something.
With reference to	Throughout your essay, link your answer to the source(s) cited in the question.

Appendix D: Deconstructing essay questions using GALA

GALA template

Essay Question:

	Question Deconstruction
General topic area:	
Aspect of general topic to be addressed:	
Limiting word(s):	
Action word(s):	

Example 1

Essay Question: *Assess the contribution trade unions make to society.*

	Question Deconstruction
General topic area:	*trade unions*
Aspect of general topic to be addressed:	*contribution they make*
Limiting word(s):	*to society*
Action word(s):	*Assess: estimate the worth/value of something by weighing up the advantages and disadvantages or strengths and weaknesses or arguments for and against.*

Reinterpretation of essay question in light of definition of action word:

> *Estimate the contribution made by trade unions to society (weighing up the pros and cons).*

Example 2: Compare

Essay Question: *Compare Australasian and North American approaches to funding universities.*

	Question Deconstruction
General topic area:	*universities*
Aspect of general topic to be addressed:	*funding*
Limiting word(s):	*Australasian and North American approaches*
Action word(s):	*Compare*: show similarities and/or differences where they exist.

Reinterpretation of essay question in light of definition of action word:

> *Show the similarities and differences between the Australasian and North American approaches to funding universities.*

Although the action word *compare* leans towards showing similarities between things (e.g. 'compare and contrast'), where differences exist they also ought to be highlighted. This reflects common usage of the word 'compare', which ordinarily is interpreted to mean to look at two things in the round.

Example 3: Contrast

Essay Question: *Contrast life expectancies for those in long-term employment against those unemployed long-term.*

	Question Deconstruction
General topic area:	*employed and unemployed*
Aspect of general topic to be addressed:	*life expectancies*
Limiting word(s):	*long-term*
Action word(s):	*Contrast*: show differences.

Reinterpretation of essay question in light of definition of action word:

> *Show the different life expectancies for those in long-term employment against those unemployed long-term.*

Example 4: Compare and contrast

Essay Question: *Compare and contrast the sporting achievements of women and men over the period covering the last three Olympic Games.*

	Question Deconstruction
General topic area:	*women and men*
Aspect of general topic to be addressed:	*sporting achievements*
Limiting word(s):	*last three Olympic Games*
Action word(s):	*Compare and contrast*: show similarities and differences.

Reinterpretation of essay question in light of definition of action word:

> *Show the similarities and differences between the sporting achievements of women and men over the period covering the last three Olympic Games.*

Although the action word *compare* could be used to elicit an answer that shows similarities and differences between the sporting achievements of men and women, *compare and contrast* is used for emphasis.

Example 5: Consider

Essay Question: *Consider the benefits, or otherwise, of group-work in student assignments.*

	Question Deconstruction
General topic area:	*group-work*
Aspect of general topic to be addressed:	*benefits, or otherwise,*
Limiting word(s):	*student assignments*
Action word(s):	*Consider*: think about and give your reasoned viewpoints, arriving at a justified conclusion.

Reinterpretation of essay question in light of definition of action word:

> *Think about, and give your reasoned viewpoints, arriving at a justified conclusion, on the benefits, or otherwise, of group-work in student assignments.*

Example 6: Critique

Essay Question: *Give a critique of Freud's model of personality.*

	Question Deconstruction
General topic area:	*Freud*
Aspect of general topic to be addressed:	*model of personality*
Limiting word(s):	–
Action word(s):	*Critique*: an in-depth, informed and balanced discussion on the merits or otherwise of something.

Reinterpretation of essay question in light of definition of action word:

> *Give an in-depth, informed and balanced discussion on the merits or otherwise of Freud's model of personality.*

Example 7: Demonstrate

Essay Question: *Demonstrate the practical problems of regulating the financial sector.*

	Question Deconstruction
General topic area:	*financial sector*
Aspect of general topic to be addressed:	*regulating*
Limiting word(s):	*practical problems*
Action word(s):	*Demonstrate*: convince using clear explanations and examples.

Reinterpretation of essay question in light of definition of action word:

> *Convince, using clear explanations and examples, the practical problems of regulating the financial sector.*

Appendix E: Feedback sheets

Typical tutor feedback form outline structure

FEEDBACK SHEET	
STUDENT NUMBER:	**MARK (/100):**
ASSIGNMENT NUMBER:	

WHAT YOUR GRADE MEANS

70+:	Distinction.	Categorised by in-depth analysis ...
60+:	Very good.	A balanced essay covering most aspects ...
50+:	Good.	A competent answer that ...
40+:	Basic pass.	Limited in a number of key areas ...
<40:	Fail.	This fails to address ...

MARKER COMMENTS

RECOMMENDATIONS FOR IMPROVEMENT

Tutor signature: **Date:**

Student notes on formal tutor feedback
(to be attached to tutor feedback)

NOTES ON FORMAL TUTOR FEEDBACK

ESSAY QUESTION:

Grade/Mark:

Date:

Strengths	Weaknesses	For Next Submission ...

Index